Study Guide for

Kahane's LOGIC AND PHILOSOPHY, 4th edition

Harrison Hall
University of Delaware

Wadsworth Publishing Company
Belmont, California
A division of Wadsworth, Inc.

Preface

This study guide is designed to accompany the fourth edition of Logic and Philosophy by Howard Kahane. It contains further discussion of topics which are especially difficult or important in sentential and predicate logic, that is, the material covered in the first two parts of that text.

The chapters in this study guide correspond exactly to the first eight chapters of Logic and Philosophy. It is important for you to read the material in the text and try to do the appropriate exercises before making use of the corresponding material contained herein. Each chapter of this study guide extends the discussion of particular topics from the text, provides answers and comments for selected problems from the exercises in the text, and gives you additional exercises where further practice might be especially helpful in learning the concepts or acquiring the skills introduced in the chapter.

CHAPTER ONE

Sentential Logic   Introduction

1   Truth and Validity

The discussion of the relationship between truth and validity in Section 5 of the text is very important. Truth and falsity are properties of sentences, not of arguments. Individual sentences in an argument (the conclusion or one of the premises, for example) are true or false, but it makes no sense to speak of arguments as being true or false. Validity and invalidity, on the other hand, are properties of arguments, not of sentences. Arguments and argument forms are the only things that can be described as valid or invalid. So the first thing to keep in mind about truth and validity is that these concepts apply to very different kinds of things.

As far as truth is concerned, we can make a distinction between the actual truth value of a sentence (whether it is in fact true or false) and the truth conditions of a sentence (what things would have to be like in order for the sentence to be true or false). Consider, for example, the sentence: "Your instructor is purple." There is no difficulty in determining its actual truth value. Unless you have a very strange instructor, the sentence is clearly false. But we can still talk about its truth conditions, that is, the conditions under which it would be true, whether it is in fact true or false. And those conditions are also fairly easy to determine. We know how things would have to be in order for that sentence to be true, namely, things would have to be such that the actual color of your instructor were purple. Of course, things aren't that way and that is why the sentence is false. The truth value of a sentence is determined by its truth conditions and by the way things actually are in the world. The truth of a sentence (its actual truth value) and the truth conditions of a sentence refer to entirely different things.

Once we have distinguished between the truth of a sentence and the truth conditions of a sentence, the second thing to keep in mind about truth and validity can be put as follows. The validity of an argument has nothing to do with the truth of any of the sentences it contains. Validity is a matter of form and not of fact or content, of truth conditions of sentences in an argument, not of their actual truth values. The premises of a valid deductive argument may be true or false. Its conclusion may be true or false. To say that it is valid is just to say that if its premises were true, then its conclusion would have to be true as well. The conditions under which all of its premises would be true include the conditions under which its conclusion would also be true.

The only combination of actual truth and falsity that validity rules out is this: a valid argument cannot have true premises and a false conclusion. Any other combination is possible. (And, of course, every combination is possible for an invalid argument.)

Every sentence in a valid argument could be false, for example:

    1. All cats are purple.
    2. Your instructor is a cat.
Therefore 3. Your instructor is purple.

What makes this argument valid is its form. Each sentence is in fact false, but if the first two were true, then the third one would have to be true also. Substituting systematically in that argument for "cats", "purple" and "your instructor" will preserve its form and produce an indefinite number of valid arguments. Some will have true premises, some false. Some will have a true conclusion, some false. The only thing that will never occur is a substitution into that form with true premises and a false conclusion. That is the one thing that the form rules out, and that is what deductive validity is all about.

Invalidity has absolutely no connection with the truth or falsity of any sentence in an argument, and rules out no combination of truth values whatsoever. Invalidity is entirely a matter of form and places no restrictions on the actual truth values of the sentences in an argument. So an invalid argument could perfectly well have all true premises and a true conclusion, for example:

    1. This is a study guide.
    2. You are a person.
Therefore 3. Your instructor's telephone is black (or whatever its
                                       true color is).

All of the above sentences are true. What makes the argument invalid is its form. The truth of the first two sentences (the premises) does not make the third sentence (the conclusion) true; and it is that relation (premises, if true, making the conclusion true) that validity requires. The third sentence happens to be true, but it would have been perfectly possible for this to be a study guide and you a person, but your instructor's telephone to be some other color. It is that possible combination that makes the argument invalid.

Exercises for Chapter One

(Note: Answers--and brief explanations, where appropriate--for the even-numbered questions and problems for all of the exercises in this study guide are available at the end of the book.)

Exercise 1-1 (Basic Concepts)

1. Can an invalid deductive argument:
    a. have true premises?
    b. have a true conclusion?
    c. have true premises and a true conclusion?
    d. have true premises and a false conclusion?
    e. be sound?

2. Can a valid deductive argument:
    a. have a false conclusion?
    b. have false premises?
    c. have false premises and a false conclusion?
    d. have true premises and a false conclusion?
    e. be unsound?

3. Must the conclusion of a valid deductive argument:
    a. be true?
    b. be true if the premises are true?
    c. be false if the premises are false?

4. Can a sound deductive argument:
    a. be valid?
    b. be invalid?
    c. have a false premise?
    d. have a false conclusion?

Exercise 1-2 (Argument Forms)

Each of the following is a valid deductive argument, having one of the following valid argument forms:

        a)   1. If _____, then ....
                    2. _____.
            Therefore 3. ....

b)   1. If _____, then ....
           2. It is not true that ....
  Therefore 3. It is not true that _____.

c)   1. Either _____ or ....
           2. It is not true that _____.
  Therefore 3. ....

d)   1. Either _____ or ....
           2. It is not true that ....
  Therefore 3. _____.

e)   1. If _____, then ....
           2. If ...., then ,,,,,,,,, .
  Therefore 3. If _____, then ,,,,,,,,, .

For each argument below, indicate which one of the above forms is a form of the argument.

1.   1. If John passes all of his courses, then he will
              graduate this semester.
           2. Unfortunately, John will not graduate this semester.
  Therefore 3. John will not pass all of his courses.

2.   1. If John does not pass all of his courses, then he
              will not graduate this semester.
           2. If he does not graduate this semester, then his
              parents will not continue to support him.
  Therefore 3. If John does not pass all of his courses, then his
              parents will not continue to support him.

3.   1. Either John will graduate this semester or he
              will have to sell used cars for a living.
           2. But John will not graduate this semester.
  Therefore 3. John will have to sell used cars for a living.

4.   1. If Jane is interested in sentential logic, then
              Tarzan will be too.
           2. Jane is interested in sentential logic.
  Therefore 3. Tarzan is interested in sentential logic too.

5.   1. Either Tarzan will do well on this exercise or
              Jane will lose some of her respect for him.
           2. But Jane will not lose any of her respect for
              Tarzan.
  Therefore 3. Tarzan will do well on this exercise.

6. 1. If Art was a junior last year, then he must be a senior now.
    2. And if he is a senior now, then he will be a graduate next year.
    Therefore 3. If Art was a junior last year, then he will be a graduate next year.

7. 1. If Art was a junior last year, then he would be a senior now.
    2. But Art is not a senior now.
    Therefore 3. Art was not a junior last year.

8. 1. Either Art or Betsy will graduate this year.
    2. However, Art will not graduate this year.
    Therefore 3. Betsy will graduate this year.

9. 1. If Art goes on to graduate school, then Betsy will too.
    2. But Betsy is not going on to graduate school.
    Therefore 3. Art is not going on to graduate school either.

10. 1. If Betsy had taken this logic course last year, then she would not be taking it now.
    2. Betsy did take this logic course last year.
    Therefore 3. Betsy is not taking this logic course now.

CHAPTER TWO

Sentential Logic--I

1 Truth-functional Meaning and Connectives

It is important that you understand what is meant by "truth-functional". This concept is discussed briefly in Section 2 of the text and defined at the end of the chapter. When we translate sentences from natural language (English in this case) into the symbolic notation introduced in this chapter, we do not preserve all of their features. We lose some of the nuances, some of the things that might be included as part of their meaning. There is one thing that we always preserve, however, and that is their truth-functional meaning. In other words, the truth of any sentence in symbolic notation is the same function of the truth of its component atomic sentences as was the English sentence it translates. For example:

> Snow is white, and coal is black.
> Snow is white, but coal is black.
> Although snow is white, coal is black.
> In spite of the fact that snow is white, coal is black.
> Snow is white, while coal is black.
> Snow is white; nevertheless, coal is black.

are all translated in symbolic notation by $S \cdot C$ (where S = Snow is white, and C = Coal is black), not because they have exactly the same meaning in English, but because they all have the same truth-functional meaning. The truth value of each is the same function of the truth values of its two atomic sentence parts; namely, each sentence above is true just in case the sentence "Snow is white" is true and the sentence "Coal is black" is also true. And those same truth conditions hold for the compound sentence $S \cdot C$ in symbolic notation. We don't need any more of the meaning of English sentences than this for purposes of logic, since the validity of deductive arguments is a function of the truth conditions of their premises and conclusions alone.

We call the connectives used in this symbolic notation truth-functional because they capture only the truth-functional meaning of the connective words or phrases in the English sentences they are used to translate. For this reason, the closest we can come to saying what the connectives themselves mean (that is, to defining them) is to give a truth table showing how the truth value of any compound sentences containing them depends on the truth values of the smaller sentences they connect.

7

2 Sentences and Sentence Forms

The relationship between sentences and sentence forms discussed in Section 7 of the text, and the ability to recognize that relationship which is tested in Exercise 2-2, are both important and quite difficult to master. The ability to identify the possible forms of particular sentences is part of the ability needed to construct proofs of validity for deductive arguments (which we begin in Chapter Four of the text). The following suggestions for checking whether forms and sentences match in particular cases may help you to recognize and understand the relationship between sentences and sentence forms.

A sentence form is a form of a given sentence if and only if there is some interpretation of its variables, (that is, some assignment of sentences to each sentence variable in the form), such that under that interpretation (that is, when those sentences are substituted systematically for those variables) the form becomes the given sentence with which you started. So, for example:

(1) p is a form of the sentence ~A, because if you
    assign the sentence ~A to the variable p and
    substitute ~A for p in the form, the result is
    exactly the sentence ~A with which you started.

(2) ~p is not a form of the sentence A, because
    there is no sentence which could be assigned to
    p such that substituting it in the form (that is,
    putting a negation sign in front of it) would
    give you exactly the sentence A as a result.

Sentence variables are much like variables in mathematics. Just as x or y or z could represent any number, so p or q or r could stand for any sentence whatsoever, atomic or compound, negated or not negated. To check the correspondence between a sentence and a form you must attempt to turn the form into the sentence (not the other way around) by 'plugging in' the values (sentences) of all its variables. The form fits the sentence only if there is some value for each of its variables which turns the form into the sentence. If the sentence to be 'plugged in' for a particular variable is compound, you will need to put parentheses around it before substituting it for the variable in the form. If you have to add anything more than parentheses around such compound sentences, or do anything else to make the form look like the sentence after substitution for its variables, then the form and sentence do not match. The form - sentence relation is one of picturing under some interpretation of the variables. It is not a matter of truth conditions or meaning. So, for example, A and ~~A do not have all the same forms (are not pictures of each other), even though they are obviously equivalent in terms of truth conditions or meaning.

There is one more thing which may be of further help. And that is showing you what it would be like to identify all the possible forms of a given sentence. The idea is that at each point in the following progression we capture more of the internal structure of the compound sentence with which we start. I will use number 7 from Exercise 2-2 in the text as my example:

$$\sim[(A \lor B) \supset C]$$

First, if we ignore all of its structure, it is still a sentence, so one of its forms will show just that. It is:

$$p$$

What kind of sentence is it? It is a negation. The initial negation sign is its major connective (that is why everything else is in brackets). So the form that picks up that feature of it is:

$$\sim p$$

The next question to ask is "What kind of sentence is being negated?" The answer is a conditional sentence--material implication is the major connective of the sentence in brackets. So we can represent the negated sentence as a conditional:

$$\sim(p \supset q)$$

The only internal structure of the conditional sentence in brackets is in its antecedent. It is a conditional sentence with a disjunction as its antecedent, and so can be represented as:

$$\sim[(p \lor q) \supset r]$$

At this point we have captured all of the structure of the original sentence. Both disjuncts are atomic, as is the consequent of the bracketed conditional, so there is no more structure to be represented.

Once we have done this, we know that every one of the infinite number of possible forms of the sentence will either be one of those on our list:

$$p$$
$$\sim p$$
$$\sim(p \supset q)$$
$$\sim[(p \lor q) \supset r]$$

or else a form obtained from one of those by systematically substituting one variable for another in one of the forms on our list. For example, since p is a form of the sentence, q or r or any other single variable would also be.

If you can do what I have done above for any sentence, you will not have any trouble matching sentences and forms. If you find that you are still having trouble with Exercise 2-2 after careful study, look at the discussion of that exercise in the next section.

Discussion of Exercises from Text

Exercise 2-1

Remember that the answers in the back of the text are for the even-numbered problems only. So when the book says that 2, 6 and 10 are conjunctions, it means that of problems 2, 4, 6, 8 and 10, only 2, 6 and 10 are correctly symbolized as conjunctions.

Of the odd-numbered problems, all are conjunctions except 3. If 3 is treated as the conjunction of two atomic sentences, the fact that Bonny and Eugene are classmates of each other is lost, and so the conjunction is not equivalent in meaning to the original sentence. The test for conjunction is whether you can split the sentence into two sentences doing nothing more than dropping the connective word(s), changing the number of the verb from plural to singular, and repeating parts of the original subject or predicate where needed--without thereby losing or changing the meaning of the sentence. If you have to add predicates or qualifying phrases which are nowhere in the original sentence in order to preserve the meaning of the original sentence, then the original sentence was not a conjunction.

Exercise 2-2

The discussion of the skill required to complete this exercise in the preceding pages is fairly complete. All I can add at this point is a careful working of one of the problems with comments. I will do problem 5. The sentence is:

$$\sim(A \lor B) \supset C$$

The first two forms, p and q, being simple variables, are forms of every sentence in the universe, and so are forms of this sentence. In the first case we assign the entire sentence, $\sim(A \lor B) \supset C$, to the variable p to turn it into a picture of the sentence. In the second case we do the same with q.

The third form, $\sim p$, is not a form of the sentence because its negation covers the entire form. Our sentence is not a negated sentence. The parentheses show that its negation sign applies to only the antecedent, $(A \lor B)$, of the sentence. Once we see this we can rule out all the negated sentence forms on the list. So, in addition to c, we can also rule out f, g, m, n and o. They cannot possibly be forms of any sentence which is not negated in its entirety.

The fourth form, $p \supset q$, is a form of the sentence. If the variable p stands for the sentence $\sim(A \lor B)$ and the variable q stands for the sentence C, replacing those variables by those sentences turns the form into an exact picture of the sentence we started with. (Remember that variables can stand for any sentence.)

The fifth form, ~p ⊃ q, is also a form of the sentence. In this case, p stands for the sentence A ∨ B (which will require parentheses around it when inserted into the form in place of p) and q stands for the sentence C.

We have already eliminated the sixth and seventh (f and g) forms because they are negated and our sentence (as a whole) is not. The eighth, ninth and tenth (h, i and j) forms can also be eliminated as possible forms, but for a different reason. No matter what sentences we substitute for p and q within the parentheses in those forms, we will not be able to get back a negation sign in front of the initial parenthesis.

The eleventh form (k) is not a possible form of the sentence because it has more structure (an extra negation sign) than the sentence itself. A form can capture, at most, all of the structure of the sentence. It cannot capture more structure than is there to be captured. The attempt to turn this form into the sentence we started with would require that we find some sentence value of p such that placing a negation sign in front of that sentence gives us the atomic sentence A. And, as the earlier discussion in this study guide indicated, that is impossible.

That takes care of all but the twelfth form (l), ~(p ∨ q) ⊃ r. This is a form of the sentence (in fact, the most complete or informative form since it captures all of the structure of the sentence) because when p=A, q=B, and r=C, the form becomes a perfect picture of the original sentence.

Exercises for Chapter Two

Exercise 2-1 (Conjunctions)

Which of the following are logically compound sentences and thus correctly symbolized as conjunctions? Explain.

1. Art and Betsy are friends.

2. John is allergic to penicillin and ragweed.

3. George and Margaret are concerned about the recent outbreak of terrorism in Europe.

4. Russia and the United States are supposed to be enemies.

5. Gin and tonic is my favorite drink.

6. The Grand Inquisitor thought that freedom and bread enough for all were incompatible.

7. Peace and prosperity are admirable political objectives.

8. No one voted for Carter and Reagan in 1980.

9. Israel and Syria are fighting bitterly for control of parts of the Middle East.

10. Carter and Reagan have tried to bring about an end to hostilities in the Middle East.

11. Burns and Allen made a great comedy team.

12. Oil and vinegar is a popular dressing for salads.

13. Reagan and Bush were running mates in the 1980 election.

14. Reagan and Bush were victorious in 1980.

15. Traffic and pollution are good reasons not to live in a very big city.

Exercise 2-2 (Sentence Forms)

For each sentence on the left, determine the sentence forms on the right of which it is a substitution instance. (Remember that a sentence may be a substitution instance of several different sentence forms.)

1. A	a. p
2. B	b. ~q
3. A · ~B	c. p · q
4. ~B · A	d. ~(p · q)
5. ~(B · A)	e. ~p · q
6. ~~A	f. p · ~q
7. A · (B ∨ C)	g. p · (q ∨ r)
8. ~(A · ~B)	h. p · (~q ∨ r)
9. ~[A · (~B ∨ C)]	i. ~(p · ~q)
10. ~[A · (~B ∨ ~C)]	j. ~(~p · ~q)
	k. ~[p · (q ∨ r)]
	l. ~[p · (~q ∨ r)]
	m. ~[p · ~(q ∨ r)]

Exercise 2-3 (Sentence Forms)

Follow the instructions for Exercise 2-2 above.

1. A	a. p
2. ~B	b. ~p
3. ~~A	c. p ⊃ q
4. A ⊃ B	d. p ⊃ ~q
5. ~A ⊃ B	e. ~p ⊃ ~q
6. ~(A ⊃ B)	f. ~p ⊃ q
7. A ⊃ (B ⊃ C)	g. ~(p ⊃ q)
8. ~[A ⊃ (B ⊃ C)]	h. ~(p ⊃ ~q)
9. ~[A ⊃ (B ⊃ ~C)]	i. p ⊃ (q ⊃ r)
	j. p ⊃ (~q ⊃ r)
	k. ~[p ⊃ (q ⊃ r)]

CHAPTER THREE

Sentential Logic--II

1 Translating Sentences into Symbolic Notation

It might be helpful to divide up the translation of English sentences into symbolic notation in the following manner: first, there are some general rules of thumb for matching English connective words and phrases with the appropriate logical connectives; second, there are some exceptions to most of those rules of thumb; third, there are a few special constructions which you will need to learn how to deal with separately, rather than trying to subsume them under the general rules of thumb for the connectives involved; and, finally, there are some things to look for in English sentences which will help you to determine the appropriate grouping or punctuation of them in symbolic notation. The discussion of translation in sentential logic which follows will be divided into sections as indicated above. At the end of the discussion is a list of "translation hints" which may be helpful to you while you are in the process of acquiring this skill.

a. **General rules of thumb for associating English connective words and phrases with the apporopriate logical connective:**

In general, the English connectives on the right can be translated by the logical connective on the left.

$\sim$ (negation)   --   Sentences containing the word "not" or its equivalent "n't" are translated with an initial negation sign. If the sentence being negated is compound, it must be enclosed in parentheses to indicate the scope of the negation sign.

$\cdot$ (conjunction) --   Sentences containing the words or phrases "and", "but", "though", "even though", "although", "in spite of the fact that", "while" or "because" are translated with the symbol for conjunction between the two sentences they connect. If either of the two sentences is compound, it must be enclosed in parentheses.

v (disjunction) --   Sentences containing the words "or" or "either ...or" are translated with the symbol for disjunction between the two sentences they connect. If either of the two sentences is compound, it must be enclosed in parentheses.

⊃ (material   -- Sentences containing the words or phrases
  implication)   "if", "in case" or "if...then" are translated
                          with the symbol for material implication
                          between the two sentences and the "if..." or
                          "in case..." sentence first. If either of the
                          two sentences is compound, it must be enclosed
                          in parentheses.

≡ (material   -- Sentences containing the phrases "if and only
  equivalence)   if" or "just in case" are translated with the
                          symbol for material equivalence between the
                          two sentences they connect. If either of the
                          two sentences is compound, it must be enclosed
                          in parentheses.

( ) (punctuation) -- The 'grammar' rules which apply to our sym-
[ ]   bolic notation require that each logical
{ }   connective join exactly two sentences, with
                          no two connectives trying to join the same
                          sentence to any other sentence. So, for
                          example,

$$A \cdot B \supset C$$

is not a sentence in symbolic notation at all.
Parentheses, brackets or braces must be used
to identify which connective actually has a
hold on B, and which two sentences each of the
connectives actually joins. Either of these
is possible:

$$A \cdot (B \supset C)$$
$$(A \cdot B) \supset C$$

And those are very different sentences with
very different truth conditions.. For
instance, if A is false the first sentence
will be false and the second one true,
regardless of the truth values of B and C.

Parentheses, brackets or braces are also
required to identify the scope of a negation
sign when it negates a compound sentence.
So, for example,

$$\sim A \supset B$$
and $$\sim(A \supset B)$$

are different sentences with different truth
conditions. Without any parentheses, the
negation sign in the first sentence negates
only the atomic sentence immediately following it. With parentheses, the negation

sign in the second sentence negates the entire conditional (material implication) sentence A ⊃ B.

Both in the text and in this study guide, parentheses are used first, brackets second, and braces afterwards, whenever multiple punctuation or grouping is required within the same sentence. The following sentence illustrates this practice:

$$\sim\{A \vee [B \supset (C \equiv D)]\}$$

The only reason for this convention is to make it easier to read the sentence and identify its grouping. All three of the pairs of punctuation marks are identical in their meaning or function.

b. Exceptions to the general rules of thumb given above:

The following lists on the right the few things you need to keep in mind in order not to be misled when using the rules of thumb given above to produce the logical connective on the left.

~ (negation) -- There are no real exceptions to the rule of thumb for this logical symbol. You do need to be very careful not to miss the fact that an English sentence is negative. This feature of the sentence must be captured when it is translated into symbolic notation. Remember that a negated sentence cannot be translated by a single capital letter because capital letters can name atomic sentences only.

Although you will not encounter this often, it is possible to produce a negated sentence in English without the use of "not" or "n't" by means of constructions such as "It is false that _____", where the blank is filled in with a sentence. Such constructions should not cause you any difficulty; their meaning is clearly the same as the same sentence with "not" in it and the construction removed. Simply translate such sentences as negations.

• (conjunction) -- It might be helpful to refer back to the discussion of "truth-functional meaning and connectives" in the previous chapter of this study guide to understand why so many different English connective words and phrases are translated as conjunctions. The only exception to the rule of thumb for this connective is that occasionally the word "and" connects words rather than whole sentences.

16

When this occurs, the resulting "and" sentence is an atomic sentence rather than a conjunction. You have already dealt with this problem in the previous chapter of the text and this guide in connection with Exercises 2-1. All you need to do at this point is to keep it in mind.

v (disjunction) -- Remember that the logical connective has the same truth conditions as the inclusive "or" in English. It means either...or..., or both. As your text indicates in the previous chapter, that is usually sufficient for the validity of arguments, even when the disjunctions they contain in English actually involve an exclusive "or". And the exercises in the text which involve disjunctions are all treated as though the English sentences contained the inclusive "or" only. Still, if you want or need to capture all of the truth-functional meaning of an exclusive "or" in English (one which means either...or..., but not both), you will have to add to the disjunction in symbolic notation a translation of the "but not both" part of the meaning of the English sentence. So, for example, the sentence,

$$A \text{ (exclusive) or } B$$

would be translated,

$$(A \lor B) \cdot \sim(A \cdot B)$$

if we wanted to capture all of the truth-functional meaning of its exclusive "or".

⊃ (material implication) -- The previous chapter of the text discusses at some length the differences between the truth conditions of most conditional sentences in ordinary English and the truth conditions for this logical connective. Most English conditionals assert at least some kind of causal relationship between the contents of the two sentences involved, and so are not truth-functional at all. The logical connective captures only the one truth condition that all conditional sentences have in common. And that is, if their antecedents are true and their consequents false, the entire conditional sentence is false.

For purposes of translation in both the text and study guide, the problems with conditional

sentences just discussed can be ignored. All
conditional sentences may be translated as
though they had the same truth conditions as
do material implication sentences in symbolic
notation. That is, the general rule of thumb
for this logical connective can be treated as
though it had no exceptions.

≡ (material   -- The problems with this connective are the same
equivalence)   as those for material implication. As in the
                     case of the previous connective, these prob-
                     lems can be ignored and the general rule of
                     thumb for material equivalence treated as
                     though it had no exceptions.

     As the section above indicates, there are no special problems asso-
ciated with negations. In terms of the translations you will encounter
in the text and study guide, the problems involved in distinguishing the
two kinds of English disjunctions probably will not arise, and all
problems associated with material implication and material equivalence
sentences can simply be ignored. The one exception to the general rule
of thumb for sentences containing the word "and" is a minor one and
should already be familiar to you as a result of your work in the
previous chapter. This means that the only thing you need in order to
be able to translate virtually any sentence into the symbolic notation
of sentential logic, in addition to remembering the rules of thumb for
each connective, is to learn a few special constructions and to be
careful about the punctuation or grouping of the sentences you
translate. These last points are discussed in the two sections below.

c. **Special constructions in English and their translation:**

  "neither...nor..." -- The English connective phrase "neither...
                          nor..." is equivalent in meaning to "not
                          (either...or...)" and so can be translated as
                          the negation of the disjunction of the two
                          sentences connected. The "either...or..."
                          sentence must be enclosed in parentheses so
                          that the scope of the negation sign is the
                          entire disjunction. So, for example, the sen-
                          tence,

                          "Neither Art nor Betsy will go to the show"

                          could be rewritten as:

                          "It is not the case that either Art or Betsy
                          will go to the show"

and so can be translated as:

$$\sim(A \vee B)$$

Since the English sentence could also be re-written as:

"Art won't go to the show and Betsy won't go either"

without thereby changing its meaning, the sentence could also be translated:

$$\sim A \cdot \sim B$$

You can check the equivalence of these two translations in symbolic notation by means of a truth table containing both of them. (Truth tables and their construction are discussed later in this chapter.) The "translation hints" which appear later in this chapter list both of these ways to translate the "neither...nor..." construction.

"only if" -- The effect of the "only" in this construction is to reverse the order of the material implication. You can translate sentences containing this construction as though they contained an "if" without the "only", and then turn the translation around. So, for example, the sentence:

"You will become a billionaire only if you are careful with your money"

can be treated as the simple "if" sentence:

"You will become a billionaire if you are careful with your money"

which is itself equivalent to:

"If you are careful with your money, then you will become a billionaire"

and so can be translated in symbolic notation as:

$$C \supset B$$

If you simply turn this around as follows:

$$B \supset C$$

you will have translated the original "only if" sentence correctly. "Only if" reverses the order of the corresponding "if" sentence and can be translated accordingly.

"unless" -- Sentences containing this word can be easily translated if you simply replace "unless" by the words "if not". So, for example, the sentence:

"You will not become a billionaire unless you are careful with your money"

can be rewritten in very awkward English as:

"You will not become a billionaire if not you are careful with your money"

which can be put less awkwardly as follows:

"You will not become a billionaire if you are not careful with your money"

In standard "if...then" form this becomes:

"If you are not careful with your money, then you will not become a billionaire"

and so can be translated as follows:

$$\sim C \supset \sim B$$

The formula for translating this sentence which is contained in the "translation hints" which follow would have yielded:

$$B \supset C$$

as the translation for this same sentence. This is also correct, and coincides with the intuitive fact that this English sentence conveys the same information as does the "only if" sentence we translated above. You may check the equivalence of these two translations by means of a truth table if you wish. Since they are equivalent, you may translate any "unless" sentence by either substituting "if not" and proceeding as illustrated above, or by utilizing the appropriate formula from the "translation hints", whichever you find to be easier for you.

The discussion of a possible ambiguity in the meaning of some "only if" and "unless" sentences which is discussed on pages 31 and 32 of the text is sometimes found to be confusing. What follows is intended to give you another way to look at that material which may help you to understand the distinction being drawn and how to apply it.

The translations of "only if" and "unless" sentences suggested above capture all of the literal meaning of those sentences. However, when we use "only if" and "unless" sentences we may, in some circumstances, be taken to mean more than such sentences literally mean. For example, the sentence:

"You will pass only if you study"

means literally:

"If you do pass, then you did study"

and so would be translated:

$$P \supset S$$

But the normal context in which such a sentence would be uttered is one in which students are being motivated to study by means of their desire to achieve a passing grade. And, within such a context, it would be natural to add to the indirect motivation provided by the fact that students will not be able to pass without studying, the more direct motivation provided by the fact that students will be able to pass if they do study. And so someone uttering that "only if" sentence would frequently be taken to imply the reverse of the literal meaning of the sentence as well, that is:

"If you do study, then you will pass"

And that would be translated:

$$S \supset P$$

Thus the broader meaning of the sentence (what the sentence **literally** means plus what may be taken to be implied along with it) becomes:

$$(P \supset S) \text{ and } (S \supset P)$$

And that is equivalent to:

$$P \equiv S$$

You should produce such "broader meaning" translations of "only if" and "unless" sentences whenever the natural context in which such a sentence would be uttered suggests that more than its literal meaning is implied. Unfortunately, when you are given isolated sentences to translate, it is not always possible to tell enough about the context to know whether or not this broader meaning is appropriate. When in doubt, it is probably best to produce a translation of the literal meaning only, which you can do by following the instructions at the beginning of this section or the "translation hints" which follow.

Although there are many "only if" and "unless" sentences for which it may not be entirely clear to you whether or not the "broader meaning" translation is appropriate, there are a number of such sentences for which it is clearly inappropriate. You should learn to recognize these. There is an example of such a sentence on page 31 of the text. And if you look back at the examples which were translated at the beginning of this section, you will find that they also belong to this group. In general, these sentences can be recognized by the fact that the "literal meaning" translation produces an obviously true (material implication) sentence, while the "broader meaning" translation produces a false (material equivalence) sentence because the reverse implication is clearly false. All of these sentences must be translated as material implication sentences which capture their literal meaning only.

If you translate an "only if" or "unless" sentence literally and the answer given in the back of the text or study guide is a "broader meaning" translation, or vice versa, there may appear to be more than a difference in major connective separating the two answers, even though the major connective is the only real difference between them. Let me explain how this can occur. For material equivalence sentences (unlike material implication sentences) the order is irrelevant. Material equivalence is a symmetrical relationship, so, for example,

$$P \equiv S \text{ and } S \equiv P$$

are identical in meaning. Since what is equivalent in material equivalence sentences is the truth value on either side of the connective, you can not only turn such sentences around, you can also add or subtract a negation sign as long as you do it on both sides. So:

$$P \equiv S, \sim P \equiv \sim S, S \equiv P, \text{ and } \sim S \equiv \sim P$$

are all the same sentence in spite of the differences in appearance. So if you translated literally and the text or study guide did not, or vice versa, you may need not only to change the major connective, but to turn the equivalence sentence around and add or subtract negation signs from both sides of it (double negations are equivalent to no negation and can be dropped) as well in order to see the real relationship between the two answers.

d. Punctuation or grouping of compound sentences:

In general, the first connective words or phrases which occur in an English sentence correspond to the major connective of the entire sentence. The sentences on either side of this connective will need to be enclosed in parentheses, brackets or braces if they are themselves compound. The correct punctuation or grouping of the rest of the sentence can usually be determined by applying this same rule to the parts of the original sentence on each side of the major connective.

The punctuation of a sentence in English is also a good guide to its proper grouping in symbolic notation. More major punctuation of the sentence in English tends to indicate its more major connective. If a compound sentence has a single comma, that will most likely identify the grouping around its major connective, with everything preceding the comma on one side and everything following it on the other side of that connective. If an English sentence has commas and a semicolon, the semicolon probably separates the sentence around its major connective.

If all else fails, or if the suggestions above lead to conflicting groupings of the same sentence, your intuitions about what the sentence means in English will have to guide you in deciding how to punctuate it so as to accurately represent its truth conditions.

There are two last things you should note concerning translation in sentential logic. First, the symbolic notation used greatly oversimplifies the structure of our natural language. Not only do we miss any meaning which is not truth-functional, but we also lose things like tense, voice and mood. That is why I was able in the discussion above to translate the same sentence from symbolic notation back into English indifferently as "you study" and "you did study", or, in another case, "you do pass" and "you will pass".

Second, you may translate sentences (other than the special "only if" and "unless" sentences discussed above) differently than they are translated either in the text or this study guide, and still be correct. The rule is that any formula which is logically equivalent to a correct translation of the sentence is itself a correct translation. Unfortunately, that isn't much help to you until you have mastered the argument forms from the last part of Chapter Four of the text so that you can check for logical equivalence. There is one thing you can do now, however, to test the equivalence of two sentences in symbolic notation. You can construct truth tables for the two sentences with identical atomic sentence columns in each (see the next section of this manual for the construction of truth tables). If the final column of each truth table is the same as the other, then the two sentences are equivalent; if not, they are not.

The "translation hints" whioh follow should be much more than you will need to memorize in order to translate sentences from English into symbolic notation without much difficulty. Many of them can be eliminated if you will transform English sentences into a kind of standard form before worrying about translating them into symbols. For example, if you transform:

and   "You will pass if you study"
           "If you study, you will pass"

into   "If you study, then you will pass"

you would need only one instead of three different translation formulas, namely:

If p, then q ------ $p \supset q$

Also, with practice, many of these formulas will become second nature to you and will not need to be memorized. The point of providing all of them is so that you will have them to memorize for any kinds of sentences that give you persistent trouble when you try to translate them using only your intuitions.

Translation Hints for Sentential Logic

1. Look for the overall form (the major connective) of a sentence first, regardless of the complexity of its component parts; then do the same with the parts, and so on.

2. Introductory words and phrases such as "anyway", "similarly", "nonetheless", "surely", "in fact", "of course" and so on have no truth-functional meaning whatsoever, and so can be ignored entirely when translating English sentences into symbolic notation.

3. In general, translate the following words or phrases on the left by the connectives indicated to produce the sentence patterns given on the right.

i. negation
    (a) It is not true that p ------- ~p

    (b) It is not the case that p --- ~p

    (c) It is false that p ---------- ~p

ii. conjunction
    (a) p and q -------------------- p · q

    (b) p but q -------------------- p · q

    (c) although p, q --------------- p · q
        (though)
        (even though)

    (d) because p, q --------------- p · q

    (e) both p and q --------------- p · q

    (f) in spite of the
        fact that p, q ----------- p · q

    (g) while p, q ------------------ p · q

iii. disjunction
    (a) either p or q --------------- p ∨ q

    (b) p or q --------------------- p ∨ q

    (c) neither p nor q ------------- ~(p ∨ q) or
                              ~p · ~q

iv. material
  implication (a) if p, then q ---------------- $p \supset q$

        (b) in case p, q ---------------- $p \supset q$

        (c) p if q --------------------- $q \supset p$

        (d) p in case q ---------------- $q \supset p$

        (e) p only if q ---------------- $p \supset q$

        (f) only if p, q ---------------- $q \supset p$

        (g) not p unless q -------------- $p \supset q$ or
                         $\sim q \supset \sim p$

        (h) p unless q ------------------ $\sim p \supset q$ or
                         $\sim q \supset p$

        (i) unless p, q ---------------- $\sim p \supset q$

v. material
  equivalence (a) p if and only if q ---------- $p \equiv q$

        (b) p just in case q ------------ $p \equiv q$

2   Truth Tables and Truth Table Analysis

The discussion of truth table analysis in the second section of this chapter of the text should be all that you need in order to understand how this technique works. What this technique does, in effect, is allow you to produce one row of a complete truth table very quickly--that is, without having to produce the rest of the truth table. For example, if we know that A is false, B is true, and C is false, we can find the truth value of the compound sentence:

$$(A \cdot B) \supset (B \equiv \sim C)$$

by using truth table analysis as illustrated below.

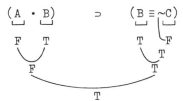

What we have done above is work downward from the truth values of the atomic sentence parts to the truth value of the whole sentence, using our understanding of the truth conditions of the logical connectives to make each individual step.

In this chapter of the text, truth table analysis is used for more than the purpose illustrated above. It is also used to determine all of the truth conditions of a given sentence or form, that is, to produce the entire final column of a complete truth table for the sentence or form in question. You will find that when a sentence or form is fairly complex (for example, those in the last half of Exercise 3-5 in the text), this method is not very satisfactory. It becomes very difficult to tell whether you have exhausted all the possible combinations of truth values for the atomic sentences (or variables) involved, and there are many opportunities for careless mistakes to occur in between atomic sentences (or variables) and the truth value of the entire sentence (or form) at this level of complexity.

When you need to determine all of the truth conditions of a given sentence (or form), I recommend that you produce a complete truth table for the sentence (or form), rather than try to make the shortcut technique of truth table analysis suffice. All of the truth tables in the text are complete in the sense of showing the truth value of the entire sentence (or form) for all possible combinations of truth values of its atomic sentence (or variable) parts. But these tables are not complete in the sense of showing the truth conditions of all of the compound parts of the entire sentence (or form) so that you can see where the final column comes from and what makes it correct. A recipe for mechanically constructing truth tables which are complete in both of these senses is as follows:

(1) Count the number of **different** atomic sentences in the compound sentence. I will call this number n.

(2) The length of the truth table will be 2^n rows (that is, 2^1 or 2 rows if there is only one atomic sentence, 2^2 or 4 rows if there are 2, 2^3 or 8 rows if there are 3, and so on).

(3) Let the first n columns from the left of the table be columns for each of the n different atomic sentences (in any order).

(4) Construct additional columns to the right for every compound sentence which is a smaller part of the whole sentence for which the table is being constructed. Arrange them from left to right so that they go from less to more complex, if possible.

(5) The final column (on the right) of the truth table will be the column for the entire sentence for which the table was constructed.

(6) Fill in values for the first n columns (the atomic sentences) as follows:

   a. Divide the first column in half. Put T's in the top half and F's in the bottom half of this column.

   b. Divide the second column (if there is one) into fourths. Put T's in the top fourth, F's in the next, T's in the next, and F's in the bottom fourth.

   c. Divide the third of the first n columns (if there is one) into eighths. Put T's in the top eighth, F's in the second, and so on.

   d. Divide the fourth column (if there is a fourth atomic sentence) into sixteenths and do the same as above.

   e. And so on... When you are done with the first n columns, the last one of them should alternate T, F, T, F, etc.

(7) If you have constructed the table correctly, each column to the right of the first n can be filled in by looking at one (if it is a negated sentence) or two (if its major connective is not negation) previous columns and filling in the new column as required by the truth conditions of its major connective.

So, full truth tables for these sentences would be as follows:

For ~A:

A	~A
T	F
F	T

For A · B:

A	B	A · B
T	T	T
T	F	F
F	T	F
F	F	F

For A ⊃ (A ∨ B):

A	B	A ∨ B	A ⊃ (A ∨ B)
T	T	T	T
T	F	T	T
F	T	T	T
F	F	F	T

For (A · B) ⊃ (B ≡ ~C):

A	B	C	~C	A · B	B ≡ ~C	(A · B) ⊃ (B ≡ ~C)
T	T	T	F	T	F	F
T	T	F	T	T	T	T
T	F	T	F	F	T	T
T	F	F	T	F	F	T
F	T	T	F	F	F	T
F	T	F	T	F	T	T
F	F	T	F	F	T	T
F	F	F	T	F	F	T

29

3 Tautologies, Contradictions, and Contingent Sentences

The discussion of tautologies, contradictions and contingent sentences in the third section of this chapter of the text is done almost entirely in terms of sentence forms rather than sentences. It is important to remember that while every sentence which has a tautologous or contradictory sentence form as one of its forms is a tautology or a contradiction, a sentence which has a contingent sentence form as one of its forms may be either a tautology, a contradiction, or a contingent sentence. A contingent sentence is one which has only contingent sentence forms as possible forms of it.

Below are pairs of definitions for each of the three kinds of sentences which do not refer to their forms at all. In each case, the first definition of the pair is the more theoretical; the second is more practical and gives you a way to identify just those sentences which satisfy the first definition.

A tautology (or tautologous sentence) is:

    (1) a compound sentence which is true regardless of the truth values of its component atomic sentences.

    (2) a compound sentence whose truth table has all T's in its final column.

A contradiction (or contradictory sentence) is:

    (1) a compound sentence which is false regardless of the truth values of its component atomic sentences.

    (2) a compound sentence whose truth table has all F's in its final column.

A contingent sentence is:

    (1) a sentence which can be either true or false, depending upon the truth values of its component atomic sentences (or upon its own truth value if it is itself an atomic sentence).

    (2) a sentence whose truth table has at least one T and at least one F in its final column.

Notice that only compound sentences can be tautologous or contradictory. All atomic sentences are contingent. But compound sentences can be contingent as well.

Discussion of Exercises from Text

Exercise 3-1

For the most part, the discussion of punctuation or grouping in this chapter of the study guide will lead you to the correct grouping of these sentences. There are, however, two exceptions. In sentence 8, the punctuation of the English sentence gives you no information about its grouping. And the first English connective word does not indicate the major connective of the sentence. To get the correct grouping for this sentence, you have to fall back on your intuitions as a native speaker of English about what information such a sentence would typically be used to convey. Sentence 13 is the other possible problem in terms of grouping. The first English connective word will give you the sentence's major connective, but you must be careful not to misidentify the "but" with which the sentence begins as its first connective word. That "but" is being used as a non-truth-functional introductory word, just like those referred to in the "translation hints", and is not a connective word at all in this sentence. If you ignore it entirely, the sentence is not very difficult to translate.

Some of the sentences in this exercise are fairly long and complex, but none of them are really difficult if you group them correctly and follow the "translation hints" from this chapter. Remember, as the earlier discussion indicated, that there is more than one correct translation for most of these sentences. So, for example, if you translated the "neither...nor..." construction differently, you would get $(R \cdot A) \vee \sim(R \vee A)$ for sentence 2 instead of the answer in the back of the text.

Exercise 3-2

Remember that you do not have to produce exactly the same English words as those in the answers in the back of the text in order to have translated these sentences correctly. The instructions do tell you to stay close to the structure of the sentences as they are written in symbolic notation, however, and that is why, for example, the answers for sentences 4 and 6 do not involve the more natural "neither...nor..." construction. Several of the other answers could also be put into more typical English if the logical structure of the sentence in symbols were not adhered to so strictly.

Exercise 3-3

All of the sentences in this exercise belong to the class of "only if" and "unless" sentences discussed in this chapter which could be either material implication or material equivalence sentences depending upon their context and interpretation. And for most of them it is not at all clear which way that decision should go. I will run through the answers briefly below in an attempt to explain just what is at issue in each case in the decision between the literal and the broader possible meanings of those sentences.

2. This sentence clearly means at least that if Janet does not run, then Harry will not run either. And that would be translated as ~J ⊃~H, or equivalently, H ⊃ J (If Harry does run then Janet did run, because he wouldn't have run unless she did). However, if you think that one who uttered this sentence would also mean to imply that Harry will run if Janet does, then you would translate the sentence to include this as part of its broader meaning, as follows: H ≡ J, or equivalently J ≡ H, ~H ≡ ~J, or ~J ≡ ~H. See the discussion at the end of the section on special constructions in this chapter if you have questions about such equivalences.

4. This sentence clearly means at least that if Harry does not run, then Janet won't. And that would be translated as ~H ⊃~J, or equivalently, J ⊃ H (If Janet does run then Harry did run, because she wouldn't have run unless he did). However, if you think that this sentence would also typically imply that Janet will run if Harry does, then you would translate it to include this as part of its broader meaning, as follows: J ≡ H, or equivalently H ≡ J, ~J ≡ ~H, or ~H ≡ ~J.

6. This sentence clearly means that if pain does not increase, then pleasure will increase. That is what the sentence says literally. But because of our understanding of the relationship between pain and pleasure, we also know that if pleasure does increase, then pain cannot have increased. And so it is natural for us to take the sentence as carrying this additional implication as well. The literal meaning of the sentence translates as ~N ⊃P in symbolic notation. The additional implication can be translated as P ⊃~N. And those two sentences together yield the material equivalence sentence, ~N ≡ P, or, equivalently, P ≡~N as in the back of the text.

8. If you translate the "unless" as "if not" in this sentence, you will be able to see why there are two different ways of translating the sentence on the right hand side of the answer in the back of the text. This sentence would then be in the form: not (either...or...). And this is the same as "neither...nor..." and so can be translated either as the negation of a disjunction or as the conjunction of the negations of the two atomic sentences involved (with a double negation dropped) as indicated in the "translation hints" for this chapter. The sentence is translated as a material equivalence rather than a material implication sentence because of our understanding of the relationship between pain and pleasure on the one hand, and mental depression on the other. The sentence says literally that if we have more pain and less pleasure, then we will have more mental depression. But we also know that if we have more mental depression it will bring

with it more pain and less pleasure. And so we would capture both
implications by means of the material equivalence sentence. You
should note that "we'll fail to reduce" just means "we won't
reduce". And remember that, since material equivalence is a symmetrical relation, either answer in the back of the text can be
turned around without changing its meaning or, hence, its correct-
ness as a translation of the sentence.

Exercise 3-4

     This exercise tests your ability to do truth table analysis on a
range of compound sentences, and some of the sentences are quite
complex. The discussion of truth table analysis in the text and study
guide shows how this should be done. I will do one of the more complex
sentences from this exercise as a further example.

8. $[(A \supset \sim B) \lor (C \cdot \sim D)] \equiv [\sim(A \supset D) \lor (\sim C \lor E)]$

Exercise 3-5

     As the discussion in this chapter of this study guide indicated, I
recommend that you use complete truth tables rather than the 'shortcut'
technique of truth table analysis to do this exercise. You will find
doing so especially helpful with the more complex forms toward the end
of the exercise. Full instructions for constructing truth tables are
contained in this chapter, and I will do one of the forms from this
exercise as a further sample.

4. $p \supset [q \supset (p \supset r)]$ is a contingent sentence form as the truth table
    below indicates:

p	q	r	$p \supset r$	$q \supset (p \supset r)$	$p \supset [q \supset (p \supset r)]$
T	T	T	T	T	T
T	T	F	F	F	F
T	F	T	T	T	T
T	F	F	F	T	T
F	T	T	T	T	T
F	T	F	T	T	T
F	F	T	T	T	T
F	F	F	T	T	T

Exercises for Chapter Three

Exercise 3-1 (Translation)

Symbolize the following sentences, using the indicated abbreviations:

1. John will not find this sentence too difficult to translate. (D = "John will find this sentence too difficult to translate")

2. John will translate this sentence correctly if he studied very diligently. (T = "John will translate this sentence correctly"; S = "John studied very diligently")

3. John did really do the exercises on his own even though he had not studied very diligently. (R = "John really did the exercises on his own")

4. John looked at the answers in the back of the book first, and so did not really do the exercises on his own. (L = "John looked at the answers in the back of the book")

5. John did not study very diligently, did not translate this sentence correctly, and did not do well in this course--thank goodness grades aren't everything. (W = "John does well in this course"; G = "Grades are everything")

6. John will neither translate this sentence correctly nor do this entire exercise perfectly. (P = "John does this entire exercise perfectly")

7. John will not do well in this course unless he studies very diligently.

8. John will do this entire exercise perfectly only if he translates this sentence correctly.

9. John will not translate this sentence correctly even though he both studies very diligently and is doing well in this course.

10. Had John studied very diligently, he would not have found this sentence too difficult to translate.

11. John would have translated this sentence correctly if he had first looked at the answers in the back of the book.

12. John will do well in this course if and only if he both studies very diligently and really does the exercises on his own.

13. Either John will translate this sentence correctly or he will not do this entire exercise perfectly.

14. If John finds this sentence too difficult to translate or does not do well in this course, it will mean that he either did not study diligently or did not really do the exercises on his own.

15. John studied very diligently, but he still found this sentence too difficult to translate and so did not do this entire exercise perfectly.

16. John will look at the answers in the back of the book just in case he finds this sentence too difficult to translate.

17. In spite of the fact that John will both translate this sentence correctly and do well in the course, he will neither study very diligently nor do this entire exercise perfectly.

18. John will translate this sentence correctly if he has studied very diligently and does not find it too difficult.

19. If John finds this sentence too difficult to translate, then it cannot be true that he either studied very diligently or really did the exercises on his own.

20. Unless John looks at the answers in the back of the book, he will not translate this sentence correctly.

Exercise 3-2 (Translation)

Translate the following into more or less colloquial English sentences. You need not adhere strictly to the logical structure of these sentences when there is a more natural way to capture the same truth conditions in ordinary English. Let:

B = "My Buick will start"
F = "There is a flat tire on my bike"
R = "I will ride my bike"
S = "I will send my Buick back to the junkyard"
T = "My Triumph will start"
W = "I will walk"

1. B • ~T

2. B ∨ T

3. ~(B ∨ T)

4. ~(B • T)

5. ~B ⊃ T

6. ~B ⊃ S

7. (B ∨ T) ∨ R

8. ~(B ∨ T) ⊃ (R ∨ W)

9. (S • ~T) ⊃ R

10. W ≡ F

11. (B • T) • (R ∨ W)

12. [(~B • ~T) • F] ⊃ W

13. $\sim W \supset [\sim F \supset (B \lor T)]$ 17. $W \equiv [(S \cdot F) \cdot \sim T]$

14. $(W \supset F) \cdot (S \supset \sim B)$ 18. $(S \equiv \sim B) \cdot \sim (W \equiv \sim R)$

15. $(F \cdot \sim B) \supset (\sim T \supset W)$ 19. $(\sim B \cdot \sim T) \lor [\sim (R \lor \sim W) \supset F]$

16. $(\sim T \cdot \sim W) \supset [\sim F \lor (\sim S \cdot B)]$ 20. $\sim W \cdot [(\sim B \cdot \sim T) \supset (F \supset R)]$

Exercise 3-3 (Tautologous, Contradictory and Contingent Sentences)

Determine which of the following sentences are tautologous, which contradictory, and which contingent.

1. $(A \supset \sim B) \equiv \sim (A \cdot B)$ 6. $\sim (A \supset B) \supset (A \equiv \sim B)$

2. $\sim (F \lor \sim G) \cdot (G \supset F)$ 7. $(F \equiv G) \lor \sim (G \supset F)$

3. $(\sim F \cdot G) \equiv (G \supset F)$ 8. $\sim (F \supset G) \lor (\sim F \cdot G)$

4. $\sim B \supset [\sim A \supset (A \equiv B)]$ 9. $(B \lor \sim B) \supset \sim [A \supset (B \supset A)]$

5. $(A \lor \sim B) \cdot \sim (A \equiv B)$ 10. $(B \supset \sim B) \equiv (A \lor \sim B)$

CHAPTER FOUR

Sentential Logic--III

This chapter of the text is devoted to proofs of validity using the eighteen valid argument forms of sentential logic. The discussion in this study guide will be divided into two parts. In the first, the eight implicational argument forms (the first eight in the text) will be discussed and a set of "strategy hints" provided for constructing proofs of validity using these argument forms only. In the second part of this chapter, the ten equivalence argument forms of sentential logic (the last ten in the text) will be discussed. A second set of "strategy hints" dealing with these new argument forms will be provided for use in constructing proofs of validity using these ten as well as the first eight valid argument forms of sentential logic. As the discussion below will demonstrate, it is very important that you keep these two sets of argument forms separate, and keep in mind the distinctions in their usage. That is the reason for presenting them in the order in which they appear in the text and for creating this sharp division of the chapter in this study guide. The exercises at the end of this chapter are divided in the same way, and labelled appropriately. The first three exercises deal with the first part of the chapter only. The last three of the six exercises deal with the material discussed in the last part of the chapter and, since the material is cumulative in its application, involve the utilization of all eighteen of the valid argument forms of sentential logic.

1 Using the Implicational Argument Forms

The implicational (first eight) argument forms can be used only on complete lines of a proof. For example, only if a complete line of a proof is a sentence of the form $p \cdot q$, can I write on a subsequent line the sentence represented by the variable p and justify doing so by SIMP.

So this move would be legitimate:

.
.
.
.
.

n. A · B

n+1. A   n, Simp

But this move would not be:

.
.
.
.
.

n.　　(A · B) ⊃ C

n+1.　A ⊃ C　　　　　　　　　　　　n, Simp

　　　Many of the argument forms list two or three lines from which a
given line may be deduced. For example, MP allows you to deduce the
sentence represented by q from a sentence whose form is p ⊃ q and the
sentence represented by p (where p and q stand for the same sentences
throughout). The order of appearance of the lines from which another
line may be deduced is irrelevant.

　　　This means that I could write B on a line of a proof and justify it
by MP if I had A ⊃ B on some previous line and A on another previous line
of the proof, regardless of which came first (A or A ⊃ B), how many lines
separated them, where either appeared in the proof (as long as both were
there before I wrote B), or how many lines separate either of them from
the line on which I write B. So the argument forms should be read in
this way:

　　　"If there is something of the form p ⊃ q as any complete
　　　line of a proof, and the sentence for which p stands as any
　　　other complete line of the proof, I can write the sentence
　　　for which q stands as a new complete line of the proof and
　　　justify it by MP and the line numbers of those two previous
　　　lines."

for MP, and so on for all of the other valid implicational argument
forms.

　　　Students frequently wonder whether or not they need to memorize the
valid argument forms in order to construct proofs of validity. The
answer is that you need to memorize them and more, even if you are
allowed to have them available to you during exams as well as when
working on the exercises. You will not become proficient at
constructing proofs until the argument forms are 'second nature' to you.
So you need not only to memorize them, but also to practice using them
until you think according to them, instead of having to think of them,
when attempting to construct a proof of validity for a particular
argument. The kind of understanding of the valid argument forms that
you need in order to be proficient at constructing proofs in sentential
logic is roughly the same as the kind of understanding of arithmetic
that you need in order to be proficient at solving algebra problems.

There are a number of different proofs of validity for any argument. There is nothing special about the answers in the back of the text or study guide. Any series of steps made according to the valid argument forms which takes you from premises to conclusion is a correct proof of validity for an argument. If you find that your proofs, although correct, are consistently of much greater length than those for the same arguments in the back of the text or study guide, you might want to study those answers and review the "strategy hints" which follow carefully in an effort to make your proofs both shorter and easier to construct.

The following page contains a list of "strategy hints" for constructing proofs of validity in sentential logic using only the implicational argument forms. You should find these helpful in connection with Exercises 4-2 and 4-4 from the text, and Exercise 4-3 in this study guide.

Strategy Hints for Proofs in Sentential Logic
(Implicational Argument Forms)

1. Look at the form of, and the atomic sentences in, the conclusion and try to work backwards through the premises and argument forms which could produce such a conclusion.

2. Try to employ atomic sentence premises (or the negation of atomic sentences) first in constructing a proof.

3. Whenever MP, MT, DS or HS (the first four valid argument forms) can be used on the premises of an argument, do so immediately and then try to see how to get from the resulting lines and remaining premises to the conclusion of the argument.

4. Mark each of the premises as you use them. When trying to come up with intuitions about how to proceed with a proof, always try to employ those premises which you have not yet made use of.

5. Do not break down compound sentences which appear more than once in an argument. Treat them as units. It may even help to rewrite the argument on scratch paper using simple variables to replace such units, and to work with the argument in this simpler form.

6. Do not hesitate to use Add to obtain atomic sentences required for the conclusion, but missing from the premises of an argument; or to obtain disjunctions which you need in the midst of a proof from simpler sentences you already have. (Students are frequently reluctant to use Add because it looks as though you get something for nothing. If you think about the truth conditions for disjunctions, however, you will see that this is not really the case.)

2 Using the Equivalence Argument Forms

The equivalence argument forms of sentential logic (the last ten of the eighteen valid argument forms) differ from the implicational forms in two respects. First, equivalence argument forms can be used on parts of lines (as well as complete lines) of a proof. For example, the following move is perfectly all right:

.
.
.
.
.

n. $(A \supset B) \supset C$

n+1. $(\sim A \vee B) \supset C$ n, Impl

whereas a similar move with an implicational argument form (that is, doing something to part of a line only) would not be permitted. Second, each of the ten equivalence argument forms justifies moves in either direction, left to right or right to left. It is very important to keep both of these differences clearly in mind when constructing proofs of validity using all eighteen of the valid argument forms of sentential logic.

All ten of the equivalence forms need to be mastered, of course. But you will probably find DeM and Impl to be especially useful in constructing proofs, and I would recommend giving them some extra study before attempting the exercises for the last part of this chapter. Dist is not used as frequently as those two forms, but seems to be the most difficult of the equivalence forms for students to master. You may find that when you are really stuck on a particular proof, it is because you have not seen an opportunity to employ this argument form. Finally, let me make a suggestion about the use of Equiv. This form allows you to convert a material equivalence sentence into either a conjunction of two conditional sentences, or a disjunction of two conjunctions. I think that the former is almost always easier to work with; so I recommend that you always break down material equivalence sentences (when they need to be broken down at all) into a conjunction of two conditional sentences and work with those. In general, I think it is a good idea to convert anything you can into conditional sentences. Then most of the work of a proof can be done with MP, MT, HS and Contra, and these argument forms are especially easy to master.

The "strategy hints" on the following page, together with the ones from the previous page, provide a complete set for constructing proofs of validity in sentential logic using all eighteen of the valid argument forms.

Strategy Hints for Proofs in Sentential Logic
(Equivalence Argument Forms)

1. Remove the negation sign in front of any non-repeated compound sentence which is either a premise of an argument or a subsequent line of a proof. Any such sentence can be put into a form which will allow you to eliminate its initial negation sign (that is, bring it 'inside' the parentheses) by using DeM.

2. Break down material equivalence sentence premises immediately unless they are repeated elsewhere in the argument. This can be done using Equiv. As indicated in the previous discussion, I recommend that you convert such sentences into conjunctions of their conditional sentence 'parts'.

3. Whenever any atomic sentence appears in only one premise of an argument and nowhere else (that is, neither in another premise nor in the conclusion), it is irrelevant to the validity of the argument. Try to transform the premise so that this irrelevant information can be separated from the rest of the information contained in that premise and subsequently ignored. This can usually be done by using Dist and/or Simp if the major connective of the premise is "∨" or "•". If the major connective is "⊃", Impl will have to first be used to change it to "∨". If the major connective is "≡", Equiv, Impl, and Simp will have to be used first to turn the premise into two lines whose major connectives are both "∨".

4. When you cannot seem to make any headway at all with a proof, try the following as a last resort. On one sheet of paper do everything you can with the premises of the argument. Then on a separate sheet, do everything you can with the conclusion using only the ten equivalence argument forms. Compare the two lists of sentences obtained. If there is any way to get from any sentence on the first list to any sentence on the second list, you have the proof and can mechanically reconstruct it.

Discussion of Exercises from Text

Exercise 4-1

The point of this exercise is simply to help you learn the argument forms and what each one of them does when applied to specific lines of a proof. There is really no additional help that I can provide for you here, and probably none is needed. If you do find that you are having trouble with this exercise, you should review the argument forms for this section of the chapter. It is also possible that looking back at the discussion of sentences and sentence forms and the skill involved in Exercise 2-2 will be of some assistance. The same comments apply to Exercises 4-3, 4-5 and 4-6, and there will be no further discussion of them in the material which follows.

Exercise 4-2

Remember that there is more than one correct proof of validity for an argument. For example, problem 2 could be started either by using HS on lines 1 and 2, or by using MT on lines 1 and 3. In either case the proof can be completed with one step of MT after that initial move, and both proofs are correct. In the back of the text, that problem is done beginning with MT. I will show you below what the rest of the proof (beyond the premises) would look like if you had started with HS instead.

4.	$T \supset S$	1,2 HS
5.	~T	3,4 MT

I will work through problem 5 below, and try to show you what the "strategy hints" are like in practice by doing my thinking on paper.

Working backwards from the conclusion: I need to deduce C, and the only place that could come from is the first premise. To get C from the first premise I would need $A \supset B$ so that I could use MP on line 1. I could get $A \supset B$ from the third premise by MP, if I had ~D. And I could get ~D from the second premise by DS if I had ~A. And ~A is ready and waiting for me; it is the fourth premise. If I work my way back up through this thinking, it gives me the proof, starting from line 5, as follows:

5.	~D	2,4 DS
6.	$A \supset B$	3.5 MP
7.	C	1,6 MP

Again, I could have gotten a different correct proof by using HS on
lines 1 and 3, and then using MP to get the conclusion, rather than
using MP twice. All proofs are equally correct as long as you get from
premises to conclusion without misusing any of the rules (that is, the
valid argument forms). Be sure to include the justifications (line
numbers and argument forms used) after each line of your proofs.

Exercise 4-4

Problem 2 could be started either by using MP on lines 1 and 3 as
shown in the back of the text, or by using HS on lines 1 and 2. In both
cases, one more step of MP completes the proof. Notice that you will
have to use Add as the final step to obtain the D needed to complete the
proof for problem 3. Problem 4 can only be done in the manner shown in
the back of the text. No other moves are possible at any point using
only the implicational argument forms. If problem 5 looks complicated,
rewrite it as the "strategy hints" suggest by substituting p for one of
the repeating compound sentences and q for the other. The argument then
looks like this:

1. p ⊃ ~C

2. q ⊃ p

3. ~C ⊃ ~p   /∴ q ⊃ ~p

Now you should be able to see that the whole proof will require only two
steps of HS. A similar strategy will simplify problems 7, 9 and 10 as
well.

The first premise in problem 6 is of no use whatsoever. It would
help you to obtain B ∨ (R · S), but without the equivalence argument forms
from the last half of this chapter, there is no way to turn that around
so as to obtain the conclusion. And a proof is not complete until the
final line contains the conclusion of the argument (not just something
that has the same meaning). So this problem can be done in no way other
than that shown in the back of the text. In problem 8, as in several
other problems in this exercise, Add will have to be used to obtain the
antecedents of conditional premises so that MP can be used. You should
become familiar with this technique. It is a commonly needed one in
constructing proofs of validity.

Although you should be able to do problem 9 without too much
difficulty once you notice the repeating compound sentences, I will work
it for you as a sample and put my thinking on paper again.

Working backwards from the conclusion: I could get ~M · ~N from the
second premise by MP if I had ~R. And if I had ~R I could also
obtain the other part of the conclusion, Z, from the fourth premise
by DS. The only way to obtain ~R is from the first premise by MT.
And to do that, all I need is exactly what is on line 3. So the

proof, starting from line 5, is as follows:

5.	~R	1,3 MT
6.	~M · ~N	2,5 MP
7.	Z	4,5 DS
8.	(~M · ~N) · Z	6,7 Conj

Exercise 4-7

It is even more important here than in the previous part of this chapter that you become familiar with and make use of the "strategy hints" provided. For example, if you turn the first premise of problem 3 into a conditional sentence as I suggested, it is much easier to see how to come up with the rest of the proof. And, in problem 5, constructing the proof becomes much less difficult if you use Impl, Dist and Simp on the first premise to separate the useful information about A and C from the useless information about B which it contains. I will show you what that would look like below:

3.	~~A ∨ (B · C)	1, Impl
4.	(~~A ∨ B) · (~~A ∨ C)	3, Dist
5.	~~A ∨ C	4, Simp

I will leave the rest of that proof to you.

Remember to use DeM and Equiv immediately on premises that are negations of non-repeating compound sentences and on premises that are non-repeating material equivalence sentences respectively as the "strategy hints" suggest. It is no accident that such moves are the first ones made in the answers in the back of the text for problems 4, 6, 8 and 12. If you are going to become proficient at proofs such as these, following those "strategy hints" is almost a necessity.

Problem 7 deserves some discussion. The first premise needs to be broken down by DeM so that the useful information about H can be separated from the useless information about K. Then you need to notice something about the conclusion. It is a conditional sentence, L ⊃ M. Every conditional sentence is equivalent to a disjunction by the use of Impl. So the conclusion can be rewritten as ~L ∨ M. Since there is no M in the premises, this tells you that you will need to derive ~L from the premises, use Add to go from ~L to ~L ∨ M, and then use Impl to turn that disjunction into the conclusion of the argument. The proof resulting from this line of thought would be as follows:

3.	~H · ~~K	1, DeM
4.	~H	3, Simp
5.	~L	2,4 MT
6.	~L ∨ M	5, Add
7.	L ⊃ M	6, Impl

You may not have seen immediately how to construct a proof for problem 9, but working backwards from the conclusion should have given it to you as follows:

The only place from which to obtain C is from the second half of the first premise by using Simp. But before Simp can be used on C · D, C · D must be a complete line of the proof and not just part of a line. And the only way to make that sentence a complete line of the proof is to separate it from the first premise by DS, the only argument form that gives you half of a disjunction by itself. And to do that, we would need the sentence ~(A · B). As soon as you see something like that you should immediately use DeM on it to see what it is you really need to obtain. Using DeM on (A · B) yields ~A ∨~B. And all you need to do to obtain that sentence is to use Add on the second premise. The proof is as follows:

3.	~A ∨~B	2, Add
4.	~(A · B)	3, DeM
5.	C · D	1,4 DS
6.	C	5, Simp

Problem 10 requires a similar use of DeM on the antecedent of the second premise so that you can see how to get that antecedent from the other two premises of the argument.

Problem 13 involves a kind of trick, so I will work it for you and explain what is involved. The "strategy hints" from this part of the chapter should get you the following from the first premise:

3.	(S ∨~R) · (S ∨ T)	1, Dist
4.	S ∨~R	3, Simp

The difficulty is in seeing how lines 2 (the second premise) and 4 help you to derive the conclusion. Here is how it works. If you turn the disjunction on line 4 into a conditional sentence as follows:

5.	~~S v ~R	4, DN
6.	~S ⊃ ~R	5, Impl

you can then use HS on lines 2 and 6 to obtain:

7.	R ⊃ ~R	2,6 HS

Now for the trick: whenever you have a conditional sentence whose antecedent and consequent are the same except that one is preceded by a (or an additional) negation sign, you can derive the consequent. Here are the steps required to do so for the problem above:

8.	~R v ~R	7, Impl
9.	~R	8, Taut

Exercise 4-8

The first half of this exercise is not very difficult, certainly less demanding than the hardest problems from the previous exercise, as far as the proofs of validity are concerned. If you are having serious difficulty here, but did not with Exercise 4-7, it would be a good idea to check your translations very carefully. Refer to Chapter Three if necessary to make sure that you have translated these arguments correctly. A slight mistranslation can change a valid argument to an invalid one, and the associated proof from fairly easy to construct to impossible. I will make some comments on selected problems, and show you how to do a few of the more difficult proofs toward the end of this exercise.

Problem 9, much like problem 7 from Exercise 4-7, requires that you think of the conclusion as a disjunction in order to see what it is that you actually need to derive, namely, the negation of its antecedent. See the discussion of problem 7, Exercise 4-7, above if you have any questions about this.

Problem 11 can be made very short if you see that you can use CD on the premises immediately. The entire proof then requires only three steps beyond the premises.

In problem 12, it is very important that you see the opportunity to use Exp on the second premise, and understand how that enables you to turn it eventually into a conditional sentence with H as its consequent. In general, you should be alert to the following: sentences on which exportation can be used give you the opportunity to reverse the order of their antecedents by using COMM when the sentence is in the form of a single conditional sentence with a conjunction as its antecedent (see the discussion of problem 4 in Exercise 4-9 below), or to change their consequents by using CONTRA when the sentence is in the form of a conditional with another smaller conditional sentence as its consequent.

This latter is illustrated in the answer in the back of the text.

The third premise of problem 13 is not necessary, but using it does make the proof a bit shorter. If you translate the argument as follows:

1. I ⊃ (S · H)

2. ~I ⊃ H

3. I ∨ ~I   /∴ H

you can see that the third premise is tautologous, and no tautologous premise can be essential to the validity of an argument. The crucial step in the proof for this argument involves the use of Dist. I will show you two ways to get to that crucial step, one using the third premise, the other using only the first two:

4. (S · H) ∨ H   1,2,3 CD

5. H ∨ (S · H)   4, Comm

6. (H ∨ S) · (H ∨ H)   5, Dist

or:

4. ~H ⊃ ~~I   2, Contra

5. ~H ⊃ I   4, DN

6. ~H ⊃ (S · H)   1,5 HS

7. ~~H ∨ (S · H)   6, Impl

8. H ∨ (S · H)   7, DN

9. (H ∨ S) · (H ∨ H)   8, Dist

From this point it is only two steps to the conclusion of the argument. I will complete the first proof above:

7. H ∨ H   6, Simp

8. H   7, Taut

The crucial thing is to see the opportunity to use Dist. If you look at line 5 in the first set of steps above, H ∨ (S · H), you can see that H must follow, since either half of the disjunction requires it. Dist is the only way to extract that information using the eighteen valid argument forms, and you need to be ready to make use of it in such circumstances.

In problem 14, you have more information available than you need in order to complete this proof. You need to derive ~A ∨ ~B, which can then be turned into the conclusion by using Impl. And to derive that disjunction, you need only derive one of the two disjuncts. But you can derive both disjuncts by DeM as shown on line 6 of the answer in the back of the text. Sometimes students will misuse an argument form to get exactly what they need even when something more or different actually follows. For example, in this case, a not uncommon mistake would be:

     6. ~A ∨ ~B   5, DeM

And sometimes students, after deriving more than they need to complete a proof, will not be able to see how to get from that point to the conclusion. In this case, the proof could be completed from line 6 using either conjunct. The text does it one way; I will show you the other below:

     7. ~B   6, Simp

     8. ~B ∨ ~A   7, Add

     9. ~A ∨ ~B   8, Comm

     10. A ⊃ ~B   9, Impl

Problem 15 should be translated into symbolic notation as follows:

     1. A ⊃ C

     2. C ⊃ F

     3. A ∨ F   /∴ F

Of course you could have used different capital letters than those I chose to represent the atomic sentences. From the first two premises you can obtain A ⊃ F. From the third premise, with a little work, you can obtain ~F ⊃ A. From this point the problem is just like problem 13 from Exercise 4-7, discussed at some length above. A ⊃ F and ~F ⊃ A give you ~F ⊃ F by HS. From that point, the conclusion follows in three steps. They are:

     n. ~~F ∨ F   n-1, Impl

     n+1. F ∨ F   n, DN

     n+2. F   n+1, Taut

Problem 16 looks complicated, but it really isn't. If you have translated the argument correctly, the proof can be constructed almost mechanically by following the applicable "strategy hints" from this chapter.

Problem 17 involves a technique which I mentioned above in connection with problem 12 from this exercise. You must use Exp and Comm on the first premise to reverse the order of the two antecedent sentences, and then Exp again to return it to its original structure. Then MP and a series of HS steps will complete the proof quite straightforwardly. The whole proof looks like this:

1.	~R ⊃ (~W ⊃ U)	
2.	U ⊃ S	
3.	S ⊃ C	
4.	~W	/∴ ~R ⊃ C
5.	(~R • ~W) ⊃ U	1, Exp
6.	(~W • ~R) ⊃ U	5, Comm
7.	~W ⊃ (~R ⊃ U)	6, Exp
8.	~R ⊃ U	4,7 MP
9.	~R ⊃ S	2,8 HS
10.	~R ⊃ C	3,9 HS

The fourth premise in problem 18 is a tautologous sentence and, fo this reason, is irrelevant to the validity of the argument. Unlike the proof for problem 13, however, the proof in this case is slightly shorter if we simply ignore the extra premise. Using the same translation of the argument as in the back of the text, the proof, starting with line 5, would be as follows:

5.	~G ⊃ ~S	1, Contra
6.	~G ⊃ F	2,3 HS
7.	S ⊃ ~F	3, Simp
8.	~S ⊃ ~G	3, Simp
9.	~~F ⊃ ~S	7, Contra
10.	F ⊃ ~S	9, DN
11.	F ⊃ ~G	8,10 HS
12.	(F ⊃ ~G) • (~G ⊃ F)	6,11 Conj

13. $F \equiv \sim G$ 12, Equiv

    Problem 19 is quite long and quite difficult. I will go over the things you need to think about in order to come up with the proof, and then produce the proof below. I have translated the argument into symbolic notation as follows:

1. $S \supset [L \supset (G \cdot O)]$

2. $G \supset [U \supset (J \cdot M)]$

3. $\sim(B \cdot H) \supset [\sim(J \cdot M) \cdot U]$ $/\therefore (S \cdot L) \supset (B \cdot H)$

First you need to notice that Exp will turn the antecedent of the first premise into the antecedent of the conclusion. This will also allow you to use the technique described in the "strategy hints" to separate the useful information in that premise from the useless information concerning the atomic sentence O which appears nowhere else in the argument. After doing that, the result needs to be put back into the form of a conditional sentence, so that HS with the second premise is possible. Then you need to see that using Contra on the third premise will turn its consequent into the consequent of the conclusion. The last piece of the puzzle is that the messy antecedent you get after using Contra on the third premise can eventually be turned into the consequent of the second premise. The conclusion follows from that point in one step by HS. The proof, starting from line 4, is as follows:

4. $(S \cdot L) \supset (G \cdot O)$ 1, Exp

5. $\sim(S \cdot L) \vee (G \cdot O)$ 4, Impl

6. $[\sim(S \cdot L) \vee G] \cdot [\sim(S \cdot L) \vee O]$ 5, Dist

7. $\sim(S \cdot L) \vee G$ 6, Simp

8. $(S \cdot L) \supset G$ 7, Impl

9. $(S \cdot L) \supset [U \supset (J \cdot M)]$ 2,8 HS

10. $\sim[\sim(J \cdot M) \cdot U] \supset \sim\sim(B \cdot H)$ 3, Contra

11. $\sim[\sim(J \cdot M) \cdot U] \supset (B \cdot H)$ 10, DN

12. $[\sim\sim(J \cdot M) \vee \sim U] \supset (B \cdot H)$ 11, DeM

13. $[(J \cdot M) \vee \sim U] \supset (B \cdot H)$ 12, DN

14. $[\sim U \vee (J \cdot M)] \supset (B \cdot H)$ 13, Comm

15. $[U \supset (J \cdot M)] \supset (B \cdot H)$ 14, Impl

16. $(S \cdot L) \supset (B \cdot H)$ 9,15 HS

The "strategy hints" should get you as far as line 7 in the solution in the back of the text for problem 20. A review of the discussion of problem 13 in Exercise 4-7 above should take you from that point to the conclusion.

Exercise 4-9

The text warns you that some of these problems are "rather difficult". You should take that warning very seriously. My treatment of this exercise will be briefer than that of the previous two. If you are having a great deal of difficulty with these problems, you need more practice at the level of difficulty of the previous problem sets, not more discussion of these problems.

On problem 1, you should use Impl, Dist and Simp on the first premise to extract $\sim$R $\lor$ $\sim$A. If you turn that and the other two premises into conditional sentences (if you pick the wrong conditional you may need to use Contra on one of them), you will be able to obtain either the conclusion or its contrapositive, $\sim$B $\supset$ $\sim$A, by two steps of HS.

On problem 3, you should use Equiv, Simp and Contra to obtain $C \supset (A \cdot B)$ from the first premise. Impl, Dist, Simp and Impl again will yield $C \supset A$ from that. The second premise can be used to derive $E \supset C$, but it isn't easy. Use Impl, DeM, Comm, Dist, Simp, Comm and Impl in that order. From $E \supset C$ and $C \supset A$, the conclusion follows by HS.

Although you have a solution in the back of the text for problem 4, there are two pieces of strategy which are worth special attention. The first is that any conditional sentence with another conditional sentence as its consequent, that is, any sentence of the form:

$$p \supset (q \supset r)$$

gives you the option of exchanging the two antecedent sentences as follows:

$(p \cdot q) \supset r$	Exp
$(q \cdot p) \supset r$	Comm
$q \supset (p \supset r)$	Exp

So, you have two ways to use HS on such conditionals and should keep that in mind. The second piece of strategy is that whenever you have such a conditional sentence with the two antecedent sentences the same, you can eliminate one of them. That is, from any sentence of the form:

$$p \supset (p \supset q)$$

52

you can obtain the sentence for which p ⊃ q stands as follows:

$$(p \cdot p) \supset q \qquad\qquad Exp$$

$$p \supset q \qquad\qquad Taut$$

You should remember both of these pieces of strategy. They may be useful for the construction of proofs other than this one at some future time.

Problem 5 is very difficult. You must turn the bracketed part of the first premise into a conditional sentence and then use Exp to leave only its consequent as the consequent of the whole line. Depending upon what conditional sentence you obtained in the first step described above, you will be able to use HS on the transformed version of the first premise and either the second premise or the contrapositive (with double negations removed) of the third premise. Thrashing around with the result of that HS move and the remaining unused premise will eventually yield the conclusion of the argument, or its contrapositive from which the conclusion can be easily obtained.

As the "strategy hints" would indicate, you need to go to work immediately on the third premise of problem 7. Impl, DeM, Simp and DN will eventually yield P ⊃ S and S ⊃ W from that premise. Together these yield P ⊃ W. From the fourth premise and P ⊃ W you can obtain ~P. ~P will give you R and Q from the first premise, which in turn give you V ⊃ W from the second premise. The fourth premise will then give you ~V from that, and that is all you need. Add S to it and use Impl to derive the conclusion.

If you can just see how to work problem 9, you have already spent more time than you needed to on this section of the study guide. The conclusion is equivalent to (A · R) ⊃ (B · S) by Contra, so I will work toward that. Intuitions are frequently easier to come by when there aren't negated compound sentences all over the place. The "strategy hints" would suggest that the first premise be broken down as follows:

3. (A ⊃ B) · (B ⊃ A)   1, Equiv

At this point there is nothing to do but go to work on the second premise as follows:

4. ~~(A · ~R) v (A · S)   2, Impl

5. (A · ~R) v (A · S)   4, DN

Now that should make you think of Dist as follows:

6. A · (~R v S)   5, Dist

Now we can get B from the A on line 6 and the A ⊃ B on line 3. And the rest of line 6 is equivalent to R ⊃ S. But how does that help? It is time to do some more work on the conclusion. (A · R) ⊃ (B · S) can be rewritten as A ⊃ [R ⊃ (B · S)] by Exp. And all we need in order to obtain that is R ⊃ (B · S), since we can Add the ~A to it and use Comm and Impl to get A ⊃ [R ⊃ (B · S)]. Now R ⊃ (B · S) can be turned into R ⊃ B and R ⊃ S by Impl, Dist and Impl again. And B will get us the first one of those by Add, Comm and Impl. And we already know how to obtain the second, so we have the proof. Written out, the rest of it looks like this:

7.	A ⊃ B	3, Simp
8.	A	6, Simp
9.	B	7,8 MP
10.	B ∨ ~R	9, Add
11.	~R ∨ B	10, Comm
12.	~R ∨ S	6, Simp
13.	(~R ∨ B) · (~R ∨ S)	11,12 Conj
14.	~R ∨ (B · S)	13, Dist
15.	R ⊃ (B · S)	14, Impl
16.	[R ⊃ (B · S)] ∨ ~A	15, Add
17.	~A ∨ [R ⊃ (B · S)]	16, Comm
18.	A ⊃ [R ⊃ (B · S)]	17, Impl
19.	(A · R) ⊃ (B · S)	18, Exp
20.	~(B · S) ⊃ ~(A · R)	19, Contra

Exercise 4-1   (Recognizing Uses of Valid Argument Forms, Implicational
               Forms only)

For each line (other than premises) in the following proofs, state
the line or lines from which it follows, and the valid argument
form used to obtain it.

(1) 1. F ∨ H   p
    2. F ⊃ G   p
    3. ~G   p
    4. ~F
    5. H

(2) 1. M ⊃ 0   p
    2. N ⊃ M   p
    3. 0 ⊃ P   p
    4. N ⊃ 0
    5. N ⊃ P

(3) 1. (M ≡ N) ⊃ ~F   p
    2. ~H   p
    3. ~F ⊃ G   p
    4. ~H ⊃ (M ≡ N)   p
    5. M ≡ N
    6. ~F
    7. G

(4) 1. N ⊃ (~H ⊃ ~K)   p
    2. (M ∨ R) ⊃ K   p
    3. ~H   p
    4. N ∨ H   p
    5. N
    6. ~H ⊃ ~K
    7. ~K
    8. ~(M ∨ R)

(5) 1. F ⊃ G   p
    2. ~I • F   p
    3. G ⊃ H   p
    4. F ⊃ H
    5. F
    6. H
    7. ~I
    8. H • ~I

(6) 1.　M ⊃ N　　　　　　p

2.　O ∨ M　　　　　　p

3.　P ⊃ Q　　　　　　p

4.　O ⊃ P　　　　　　p

5.　O ⊃ Q

6.　Q ∨ N

(7) 1.　I ∨ J　　　　　　p

2.　(K ∨ I) ⊃ L　　　p

3.　~I　　　　　　　　p

4.　(J ∨ H) ⊃ K　　　p

5.　J

6.　J ∨ H

7.　K

8.　K ∨ I

9.　L

(8) 1.　(F ∨ ~G) ⊃ R　　　p

2.　(F ∨ ~H) ⊃ S　　　p

3.　M　　　　　　　　　　p

4.　(M ∨ N) ⊃ (F · G)　p

5.　M ∨ N

6.　F · G

7.　F

8.　F ∨ ~G

9.　R

10.　F ∨ ~H

11.　S

12.　R · S

13.　G

14.　G · (R · S)

Exercise 4-2　(Identifying Errors in Proofs of Validity, Implicational
　　　　　　　Forms only)

Find and identify the errors in each of the following proofs of
validity.

(1) 1.　R ⊃ (S · T)　　　　p

2.　R　　　　　　　　　p

3.　S ⊃ W　　　　　　　p

4.　S · T　　　　　　1,2 MP

5.　S　　　　　　　　4, Simp

6.　W　　　　　　　　3,5 MP

7.　W · T　　　　　　6, Add

(2) 1. (A · B) ⊃~C   p

    2. A   p

    3. B · D   p

    4. A ⊃~C   1, Simp

    5. ~C   2,4 MP

(3) 1. (F ∨ G) ⊃ H   p

    2. ~G   p

    3. F · (H ⊃ I)   p

    4. ~H   p

    5. F ⊃ H   1,2 DS

    6. F   3, Simp

    7. H ⊃ I   3, Simp

    8. ~I   4,7 MT

    9. H   5,6 MP

    10. H ∨ ~I   8,9 Add

(4) 1. (B ∨ C) ⊃ D   p

    2. B   p

    3. B ⊃~E   p

    4. ~E · (D ⊃ C)   p

    5. D   1,2 MP

    6. D ∨ E   5, Add

    7. ~E   5,6 DS

    8. ~B   3,7 MT

    9. ~E · D   7, Add

    10. C   4,9 MP

(5) 1. M • ~O   p
    2. M ⊃ P   p
    3. ~O ⊃ N   p
    4. P • N   1,2,3 CD

(6) 1. ~A ∨ (B • C)   p
    2. ~A ⊃ ~(C ∨ D)   p
    3. ~(C ∨ D) ⊃ E   p
    4. A • ~E   p
    5. A   4, Simp
    6. B • C   1,5 DS
    7. B   6, Simp
    8. B • A   7, Add
    9. ~E   4, Simp
    10. C • ~E   6,9 Conj
    11. (B • A) • (C • ~E)   8,10 Conj

Exercise 4-3 (Proofs of Validity, Implicational Forms only)

Using the valid implicational argument forms, prove that the
following arguments are valid.

(1) 1. B • C   (3) 1. (~M ⊃ O) • ~P
    2. [(A • B) • C] ⊃ D   2. (~M ⊃ O) ⊃ L
    3. A   /∴ D   3. P ∨ N   /∴ L • N

(2) 1. (F ∨ G) ⊃ H   (4) 1. R ⊃ S
    2. J ∨ ~H   2. (T • R) ∨ U
    3. ~J   /∴ ~(F ∨ G)   3. ~U   /∴ S • T

(5) 1. ~M ⊃ ~N

2. ~N ∨ O

3. ~M ∨ P

4. ~~N   /∴ O • P

(6) 1. (~A ∨ B) ⊃ (~C ⊃ D)

2. ~A • ~D   /∴ ~~C

(7) 1. (M ∨ N) ⊃ (~O • P)

2. L ⊃ O

3. M   /∴ ~L • P

(8) 1. ~F ⊃ (G ⊃ I)

2. ~H ⊃ G

3. ~H • ~F   /∴ I ∨ K

(9) 1. ~B • C

2. (C ∨ D) ⊃ A   /∴ A • ~B

(10) 1. R ⊃ (S • ~T)

2. P ⊃ ~Q

3. ~Q ⊃ R   /∴ P ⊃ (S • ~T)

(11) 1. F ∨ ~G

2. ~G ⊃ H

3. F ⊃ (I • J)   /∴ (I • J) ∨ H

(12) 1. P ∨ ~Q

2. R ⊃ Q

3. (S ∨ T) ⊃ ~P

4. S   /∴ ~R ∨ T

(13) 1. ~R ⊃ S

2. (T ∨ U) ⊃ (W • ~R)

3. T   /∴ S ∨ R

(14) 1. (~B ≡ C) ⊃ (~D • E)

2. ~B ≡ C

3. A ∨ D   /∴ A • E

(15) 1. ~L • M

2. (M ∨ ~N) ⊃ (L ∨ O)   /∴ M • O

(16) 1. (F ∨ G) ⊃ ~H

2. J ⊃ (K • I)

3. ~H ⊃ J   /∴ (F ∨ G) ⊃ (K • I)

(17) 1. ~A ⊃ (B ⊃ ~C)

2. ~A ∨ D

3. ~(B ⊃ ~C)   /∴ D

(18) 1. (~H ∨ I) ⊃ (F · G)

2. G ⊃ K

3. ~H · ~J   /∴ ~J · K

(19) 1. (A · C) ∨ B

2. A ⊃ D

3. ~B   /∴ D ∨ E

(20) 1. F ⊃ ~H

2. (G ∨ I) ⊃ (~J · K)

3. ~H ⊃ (G ∨ I)

4. (~J · K) ⊃ L   /∴ F ⊃ L

Exercise 4-4 (Recognizing Uses of Valid Argument Forms, Implicational
and Equivalence)

For each line (other than premises) in the following proofs, state
the line or lines from which it follows, and the valid argument
form used to obtain it.

(1) 1. (R ∨ P) ⊃ Q   p

2. ~R · ~Q   p

3. ~Q

4. ~(R ∨ P)

5. ~R · ~P

6. ~P

(2) 1. L   p

2. ~~L

3. ~~L ∨ N

4. ~L ⊃ N

5. (~L ⊃ N) ∨ ~M

6. ~M ∨ (~L ⊃ N)

7. M ⊃ (~L ⊃ N)

(3) 1. F ⊃ G   p

2. ~H ⊃ ~G   p

3. ~(~F ∨ H)   p

4. ~~F · ~H

5. ~~F

6. ~H

7. ~G

8. ~F

9. ~F ∨ (I ≡ J)

10. I ≡ J

60

(4) 1. $(M \lor N) \supset 0$ p

   2. ~ 0 p

   3. $\sim P \lor N$ p

   4. $\sim M \supset \sim Q$ p

   5. $\sim(M \lor N)$

   6. $\sim M \cdot \sim N$

   7. $\sim M$

   8. $\sim Q$

   9. $\sim N$

   10. $\sim P$

   11. $\sim Q \cdot \sim P$

   12. $\sim(Q \lor P)$

   13. $\sim(\sim\sim Q \lor P)$

   14. $\sim(\sim Q \supset P)$

(5) 1. $F \lor (\sim G \cdot H)$ p

   2. $G \supset \sim F$ p

   3. $\sim\sim F \lor (\sim G \cdot H)$

   4. $\sim F \supset (\sim G \cdot H)$

   5. $G \supset (\sim G \cdot H)$

   6. $\sim G \lor (\sim G \cdot H)$

   7. $(\sim G \lor \sim G) \cdot (\sim G \lor H)$

   8. $\sim G \lor \sim G$

   9. $\sim G$

(6) 1. $P \supset (Q \supset R)$ p

   2. $\sim(P \cdot \sim Q)$ p

   3. $Q \supset (R \supset S)$ p

   4. $\sim P \lor \sim\sim Q$

   5. $P \supset \sim\sim Q$

   6. $P \supset Q$

   7. $P \supset (R \supset S)$

   8. $(P \cdot R) \supset S$

   9. $(R \cdot P) \supset S$

   10. $R \supset (P \supset S)$

   11. $(P \cdot Q) \supset R$

   12. $(Q \cdot P) \supset R$

   13. $Q \supset (P \supset R)$

   14. $P \supset (P \supset R)$

   15. $(P \cdot P) \supset R$

   16. $P \supset R$

   17. $P \supset (P \supset S)$

   18. $(P \cdot P) \supset S$

   19. $P \supset S$

   20. $\sim P \lor S$

   21. $S \lor \sim P$

   22. $\sim\sim S \lor \sim P$

   23. $\sim(\sim S \cdot P)$

(7) 1. $I \equiv (\sim J \lor \sim I)$ p

    2. $\sim F \lor \sim G$ p

    3. $J \equiv (\sim K \lor \sim J)$ p

    4. $(H \supset G) \cdot (G \supset H)$ p

    5. $[I \supset (\sim J \lor \sim I)] \cdot [(\sim J \lor \sim I) \supset I]$

    6. $[J \supset (\sim K \lor \sim J)] \cdot [(\sim K \lor \sim J) \supset J]$

    7. $(\sim J \lor \sim I) \supset I$

    8. $\sim(\sim J \lor \sim I) \lor I$

    9. $(\sim\sim J \cdot \sim\sim I) \lor I$

  10. $(\sim\sim J \cdot I) \lor I$

  11. $I \lor (\sim\sim J \cdot I)$

  12. $(I \lor \sim\sim J) \cdot (I \lor I)$

  13. $I \lor I$

  14. I

  15. $I \supset (\sim J \lor \sim I)$

  16. $\sim J \lor \sim I$

  17. $\sim\sim I$

  18. $\sim J$

  19. $(\sim K \lor \sim J) \supset J$

  20. $\sim J \lor \sim K$

  21. $\sim K \lor \sim J$

  22. J

  23. $J \lor [H \supset (G \equiv F)]$

  24. $H \supset (G \equiv F)$

Exercise 4-5   (Identifying Errors in Proofs of Validity, Implicational
                    and Equivalence Forms)

Find and identify the errors in each of the following proofs of
validity.

(1) 1. $(A \cdot B) \vee \sim C$ p

    2. $\sim D \supset \sim B$ p

    3. $(A \vee \sim C) \cdot (B \vee \sim C)$ 1, Dist

    4. $B \vee \sim C$ 3, Simp

    5. $\sim C \vee B$ 4, Comm

    6. $C \supset B$ 5, Impl

    7. $D \supset B$ 2, Contra

    8. $B \supset D$ 7, Comm

(2) 1. $F \equiv G$ p

    2. $\sim H \vee G$ p

    3. $(F \supset G) \cdot (G \supset F)$ 1, Equiv

    4. $F \supset G$ 3, Simp

    5. $\sim F \supset \sim G$ 4, Contra

    6. $G \vee \sim H$ 2, Comm

    7. $\sim G \supset \sim H$ 6, Impl

    8. $\sim F \supset \sim H$ 5,7 HS

    9. $H \supset F$ 8, Contra

(3) 1. $R \vee \sim S$ p

    2. $\sim S \equiv T$ p

    3. $U \supset (W \cdot \sim T)$ p

    4. $(\sim S \supset T) \cdot (\sim\sim S \supset \sim T)$ 2, Equiv

    5. $\sim R \supset \sim S$ 1, Impl

63

	6.	~S ⊃ T	4, Simp
	7.	~R ⊃ T	5,6 HS
	8.	(U ⊃ W) · (U ⊃ ~T)	3, Dist
	9.	U ⊃ ~T	8, Simp
	10.	~T ⊃ R	7, Contra
	11.	U ⊃ R	9,10 HS
(4)	1.	B ⊃ (A · C)	p
	2.	A ≡ B	p
	3.	~(D · E)	p
	4.	~(C · ~D)	p
	5.	(A ∨ B) · (~A ∨ ~B)	2, Equiv
	6.	~C ∨ ~~D	4, DeM
	7.	~~D	6, DN
	8.	(B ⊃ A) ⊃ C	1, Exp
	9.	~A ∨ ~B	5, Simp
	10.	B ⊃ A	9, Contra
	11.	C	8,10 MP
	12.	~D · ~E	3, DeM
	13.	~B ∨ ~(A · C)	1, Impl
	14.	(~B · ~A) ∨ (~B · ~C)	13, Dist
	15.	~A	14, Simp
	16.	~E	12, Simp
	17.	~A · ~E	15,16 Conj
	18.	~(A · E)	17, DeM

Exercise 4-6 (Proofs of Validity, Implicational and Equivalence Forms)

Using the eighteen valid argument forms of sentential logic, prove that the following arguments are valid.

(1) 1. A • ~B

    2. ~C   /∴ ~(B ∨ C)

(2) 1. ~(F ⊃ G)

    2. H ∨ G   /∴ ~(F ≡ G)

(3) 1. ~A

    2. A ≡ B   /∴ ~(A ∨ B)

(4) 1. ~(R ∨ S)

    2. T ⊃ (R • U)   /∴ T ⊃ W

(5) 1. (A • B) ⊃ ~C

    2. A • D   /∴ C ⊃ ~B

(6) 1. M ⊃ (~N • O)

    2. N • P   /∴ M ⊃ L

(7) 1. A ⊃ (~B • C)

    2. ~B ⊃ D   /∴ A ⊃ D

(8) 1. ~F ⊃ (G • ~H)

    2. H • I   /∴ G ⊃ F

(9) 1. M ⊃ (~N • ~O)

    2. P ⊃ N   /∴ M ⊃ ~P

(10) 1. R ⊃ S

    2. ~(S ∨ T)

    3. W ⊃ (R • U)   /∴ ~W

(11) 1. ~F ≡ G

    2. F

    3. ~(H ∨ I)   /∴ ~(G ∨ H)

(12) 1. ~R ≡ S

    2. ~(~R • T)   /∴ ~(T • S)

(13) 1. (A • B) ≡ C

    2. ~(B ⊃ C)   /∴ ~A

(14) 1. (F • ~G) ⊃ (H • ~I)

    2. I   /∴ F ⊃ G

(15) 1. M ≡ ~O

2. O ⊃ ~P

3. M ⊃ N   /∴ ~P ∨ N

(16) 1. ~B ∨ (A • ~C)

2. ~D ⊃ B   /∴ C ⊃ D

(17) 1. ~R ⊃ S

2. (S ∨ R) ⊃ T   /∴ W ⊃ T

(18) 1. ~F

2. H ≡ (F ∨ G)

3. ~(G ∨ I)   /∴ H ⊃ I

(19) 1. (A • ~B) ⊃ ~C

2. (A ⊃ B) ⊃ D   /∴ C ⊃ D

(20) 1. (O • M) ⊃ (P • R)

2. O • ~R   /∴ M ⊃ N

CHAPTER FIVE

Sentential Logic--IV

The first sections of this chapter add the techniques of conditional and indirect proof to the eighteen valid argument forms of sentential logic. These techniques make a number of proofs of validity much easier and shorter than they would otherwise have been, as Exercises 5-2 and 5-4 demonstrate. Moreover, without either conditional or indirect proof, the natural deduction system for sentential logic introduced in the previous chapter would be incomplete. There would be valid arguments whose validity we could not establish using only the eighteen valid argument forms.

In the later sections of this chapter, techniques are introduced which will allow you to demonstrate the invalidity of invalid arguments in sentential logic, and the consistency or inconsistency of premises of arguments in sentential logic (or any other groups of sentences which can be accurately translated into the symbolic notation of sentential logic).

1 Validity

The basic concept of validity has been adequately discussed in the first chapter of this study guide. At this point, however, it is important to note some different ways in which arguments can come to have this concept apply to them. As you will recall, validity requires that an argument's form be such that the argument could not possibly have true premises and a false conclusion. Virtually all of the arguments you have seen up to this point are valid because their premises implicitly contain their conclusions. So, if their premises are all true, then their conclusions must be true as well since they are 'in' the premises. This is the typical way in which arguments are valid. There are, however, two other ways in which arguments can satisfy the conditions specified by the definition of "validity". Because of the contrast between these two sorts of valid arguments and the more typical kind described above, you might think of these as 'valid by default'. The first such type includes all arguments whose conclusions are tautologous sentences. If an argument has a tautologous conclusion, then its conclusion cannot possibly be false. And if an argument cannot possibly have a false conclusion, then it cannot possibly have true premises and a false conclusion. So any argument with a tautologous conclusion must be valid. Since the truth of its conclusion is guaranteed by the form of the conclusion alone, independent of the premises, the truth of any premises whatsoever will be sufficient to guarantee the truth of the conclusion. And that guarantee is all that validity requires. It is arguments of this sort which we could not prove valid using the eighteen argument forms from the previous chapter alone. Proofs of validity for these arguments require either conditional or indirect proof, that is, proof techniques which make use of the conclusion of an argument, since the validity of these arguments is a function of their conclusions alone.

The second type of 'valid by default' argument consists of all arguments whose premises are inconsistent. As this chapter of the text and a subsequent section of this chapter of the study guide explain, inconsistent premises are ones which contain contradictory information and so cannot possibly all be true. And if the premises of an argument cannot possibly be true, then that argument cannot possibly have true premises **and** a false conclusion. So any argument with inconsistent premises is valid. The guarantee of the truth of the conclusion by the truth of the premises is secure for such arguments simply because it can never be put to the test. Since the validity (by default) of this last kind of argument is a function of its premises, we can prove such arguments valid using the eighteen valid argument forms of sentential logic alone, as explained below.

Inconsistent premises are premises from which an explicit contradiction, some sentence of the form $p \cdot \sim p$, can be derived. This means that a partial proof for such arguments can be constructed which has some sentence p on one line and the negation of that same sentence on another line. From that point only two additional steps are needed to reach any conclusion whatsoever. Those steps are illustrated below:

```
        .
        .
        .
        .
        .
 n.     p
        .
        .
 n'.    ~p
 n'+1.  p ∨ conclusion           n, Add
 n'+2.  conclusion               n',n'+1 DS
```

2 Conditional Proof

It is possible to give a rationale for the use of conditional proof in terms of the valid argument forms of the previous chapter. The relation between premises and conclusion of a valid deductive argument is **exactly** the same as the relation between antecedent and consequent of a logically true conditional sentence. If the premises are true, the conclusion must be as well. If the antecedent of such a sentence is true, the consequent must be as well. Otherwise the argument is invalid, or the sentence not logically true. This means that every valid argument could be represented as a logically true conditional sentence whose antecedent is the conjunction of the premises, and whose consequent is the conclusion of the argument. So an argument with three premises (the actual number of them is irrelevant, of course) could be represented in the following way:

$$[(premise\ 1 \cdot premise\ 2) \cdot premise\ 3] \supset conclusion$$

68

If the conclusion were itself a conditional sentence, that is, a sentence of the form p ⊃ q, we could represent the argument in this way as well:

[(premise 1 · premise 2) · premise 3] ⊃ (p ⊃ q)

In terms of this last representation, what conditional proof allows us to do is to treat that conditional as equivalent to the following:

{[(premise 1 · premise 2) · premise 3] · p} ⊃ q

And the two conditionals involved here are clearly equivalent because we can go from either one to the other simply by employing Exp. So conditional proof depends on nothing more than the validity of the valid argument form Exp, and so can itself be treated as a valid argument form.

In the previous section I noted that either conditional or indirect proof is required in order to construct proofs of validity for arguments which are valid because they have tautologous conclusions. An example of such an argument and a conditional proof of validity for it are given below:

1. C   /∴ A ⊃ (B ⊃ A)

2. A   AP

3. A ∨ ~B   2, Add

4. ~B ∨ A   3, Comm

5. B ⊃ A   4, Impl

6. A ⊃ (B ⊃ A)   2-5, CP

3 Indirect Proof

The discussion of validity in Section 1 above makes it possible to provide a rationale for the use of indirect proof. In an indirect proof, adding the negation of the conclusion to the premises of an argument makes it possible to derive an explicit contradiction, a sentence of the form p · ~p. There are only two ways this could happen.

(1) The premises were themselves inconsistent, in which case any sentence follows validly from them as demonstrated above.

(2) The premises were not inconsistent, but adding to them the negation of the conclusion produced the inconsistency. That means that the truth of the premises is inconsistent with the truth of the negation of the conclusion; or, equivalently, that the truth of the premises is inconsistent with the falsity of the conclusion. But that means that the

premises cannot be true and the conclusion false, which is the definition of validity.

So whichever of the above is the case, the move from premises to conclusion must be a valid one, and that is why indirect proof may be treated as a valid argument form.

The argument with a tautologous conclusion for which we constructed a conditional proof above could also have been proven valid by indirect proof. I will give the indirect proof below, since it allows me to make a number of important points about the practical use of this proof technique.

1.	C /∴ A ⊃ (B ⊃ A)	
2.	~[A ⊃ (B ⊃ A)]	AP
3.	~[~A ∨ (B ⊃ A)]	2, Impl
4.	~~A • ~(B ⊃ A)	3, DeM
5.	~~A	4, Simp
6.	~(B ⊃ A)	4, Simp
7.	~(~B ∨ A)	6, Impl
8.	~~B • ~A	7, DeM
9.	~A	8, Simp
10.	~A • ~~A	5,9 Conj
11.	A ⊃ (B ⊃ A)	2-10 IP

This proof demonstrates several points. First, whenever the conclusion of the argument is a compound sentence, the assumed premise will require parentheses, brackets or braces around that conclusion so that the initial negation sign of the assumed premise negates the argument's entire conclusion. Second, the contradiction arrived at in indirect proof need not be an atomic sentence and its negation. Any sentence whatsoever and its negation are sufficient for an indirect proof of validity. Third, any proof at all can be done indirectly. But when you use indirect proof where conditional proof or a proof without assumed premises would be indicated, you are quite likely to leave yourself a more lengthy and difficult proof as a result.

4 Using the Techniques of Conditional and Indirect Proof

Both conditional and indirect proof are extremely powerful techniques. They can make lengthy proofs short and difficult proofs easy if used properly. But it is important to remember their limitations. They do not permit everything. In each case the choice of an assumed premise determines rigidly what can and cannot be derived. Conditional proof allows you to derive only a conditional sentence whose antecedent is the assumed premise and whose consequent is whatever sentence is on the line immediately above the line on which you use CP. So in order to use CP correctly, the conclusion of the argument must be a conditional sentence, a conjunction of conditional sentences, or a sentence which can be easily turned into one of those kinds of sentences (such as a disjunction or a material equivalence sentence). When the conclusion is or has been put into that form, there is very little choice involved in the selection of an assumed premise. For each conditional sentence you wish to derive by CP, you will have to assume either its antecedent or the negation of its consequent. No other assumed premise will be of any use. If you assume its antecedent, you will need to derive its consequent to complete the proof. If you assume the negation of its consequent, you will need to derive the negation of its antecedent before using CP, and then use Contra on the line obtained by CP in order to obtain the conclusion of the argument. The choice between these two possible assumptions should be determined by seeing which of the two possible assumed premises could be most easily used in connection with the other premises of the argument.

Indirect proof allows you to derive the conclusion by obtaining an explicit contradiction after having assumed the negation of the argument's conclusion. When using IP there is no real choice involved in the assumed premise. It is determined solely by the conclusion of the argument.

The point of the above discussion is this. Be very careful in choosing assumptions when using conditional or indirect proof. Random assumed premises are useless. Assumed premises which are not correctly related to the conclusion of the argument cannot help you to reach that conclusion and can tempt you to misuse the valid argument forms in an attempt to complete a misdirected proof.

One last word of warning about conditional and indirect proof. No proof is complete if there are assumed premises which have not been used in either CP or IP. Every assumption must be closed off (or discharged) by CP or IP before any proof is complete. That is why the lines are drawn on the side for each AP used, to mark assumptions which are still open and to indicate the order in which they must be closed off by CP or IP before the proof is completed. If you use multiple assumed premises, as in the example on p.77 of the text, you must close off (or discharge) the assumptions in the reverse of the order in which you made them. If this is done correctly, the lines enclosing the assumptions and deductions from them leading to the use of CP or IP will be embedded one within another and will not intersect. This is shown on p.77 and in the last example on p.79 of the text.

Strategy Hints for Proofs in Sentential Logic
(Conditional and Indirect Proof)

1. If the conclusion of an argument is a conditional sentence or can easily be transformed into a conditional sentence using equivalence argument forms, try using the technique of conditional proof to obtain that conditional sentence.

2. If the conclusion of an argument is a conditional sentence with another conditional sentence embedded in it as its consequent, try assuming the antecedents of both conditionals in the order in which they appear in the conclusion. See the discussion on the previous page and the examples in the text if you have any questions about how to do this.

3. If the conclusion of an argument is an atomic sentence or a negated atomic sentence (or the negation of a conjunction of such sentences), and you cannot see how to obtain the conclusion directly from the premises, try using indirect proof.

4. Whenever all else fails, try using indirect proof regardless of the form of the conclusion. You are much more likely to accidentally derive a contradiction from the premises and negated conclusion of an argument than to accidentally derive the conclusion directly from the premises of the argument. This is a much more powerful "last resort" technique than that of the previous chapter and, in effect, replaces it.

5 Invalidity of Arguments, Consistency and Inconsistency of Premises

The concepts and skills involved in the last part of this chapter are not difficult ones to learn or employ. The only difficulty usually encountered by students in connection with this material is a tendency to confuse either some of the concepts or some of the skills with each other. I will run through them briefly, but it is up to you to learn them well enough to keep them separate.

(1) Concepts:

(a) **Invalidity** is a property of arguments, **not** of sentences. It is the property of not being valid, of course. For deductive arguments, this means that it applies to any argument which **could** (logically) have true premises and a false conclusion. As with validity, invalidity has nothing to do with the actual truth or falsity of any sentence in an argument. It is a function of the form (that is the relation of its premises to its conclusion) of an argument, and applies to any deductive argument whose form is such that its premises, if true, would not by virtue of their truth guarantee the truth of its conclusion.

(b) **Consistency** and **Inconsistency** are properties of groups (or sets) of sentences. They are **not** properties of arguments. A group of sentences (for example, the premises of an argument) is consistent if it would be (logically) possible for all of them to be true, whether or not they actually are true; that is, if they contain no contradictory information. A group of sentences is inconsistent if it would be (logically) impossible for all of them to be true; that is, if they do contain contradictory information.

(2) Skills:

(a) **Invalidity:** to show that an argument is invalid you must show that it is (logically) possible for its premises to be true and its conclusion false. This means that you must show that a truth value can be assigned to each atomic sentence in the argument which will make all of the premises true and the conclusion false. Truth table analysis provides both a way to come up with such an assignment and a demonstration that the resulting assignment actually does the job--makes each sentence true if it's a premise, false if it's the conclusion of the argument. In general, the easiest way to do this is as follows:

1. Start with the conclusion. Assign truth values to its atomic sentences which make the entire conclusion false, and make these same assignments throughout the premises of the argument.

2. Look for premises which can only be made true in one way, given the assignments already made to falsify the conclusion. Continue in this way until all the premises have been made true.

So, for example, if you wanted to show the following argument to be invalid:

1. A ⊃ (B ∨ C)

2. ~B

3. C   /∴ A ⊃ B

you would start with the conclusion and make it false by assigning the truth value T to A and F to B:

$$
\begin{array}{c}
\overset{\displaystyle F}{\overset{\frown}{\underset{\text{A} \ \supset \ \text{B}}{\text{T} \quad \text{F}}}}
\end{array}
$$

This assignment already makes the second premise true:

There is only one way to make the third premise true, and that is to assign the value T to C, and this also makes the first premise true given the previous assignments, as shown below:

$$
\overset{\displaystyle T}{\underset{\text{A} \ \supset \ (\text{B} \ \vee \ \text{C})}{\text{T} \quad \text{F} \quad \text{T}}}
$$

The complete truth table analysis for the argument would look like this:

1. $\overset{\displaystyle T}{\underset{\text{A} \ \supset \ (\text{B} \ \vee \ \text{C})}{\text{T} \quad \text{F} \quad \text{T}}}$

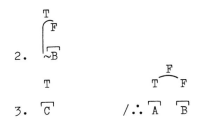

2. $\overset{T}{\underset{\sim B}{\overset{F}{\Big(}}}$

3. $\overset{T}{\boxed{C}}$ /∴ $\overset{T}{\boxed{A}} \; \overset{F}{\boxed{B}}$

(b) **Consistency**: to show that the premises of an argument (or any group of sentences for that matter) are consistent, you must show that it is (logically) possible for all of them to be true. That is, you must show that it is possible to assign a truth value to each atomic sentence in the premises which will make all of those premises true. Since this is identical to the last part of the skill just discussed, all you need to do is to ignore the conclusion of the argument entirely and proceed with the premises as indicated above under invalidity.

(c) **Inconsistency**: to show that the premises of an argument (or any group of sentences) are inconsistent, you must show that it is (logically) impossible for all of them to be true, that is, that they contain contradictory information. The way to do this is to use the valid argument forms of sentential logic to derive an explicit contradiction, a sentence of the form p · ~p, from those premises. The conclusion of the argument should be completely ignored, since the inconsistency of the premises has nothing to do with the conclusion at all.

So, for example, I could show that the premises of the following argument are inconsistent in this way:

1.	A ⊃ (B ∨ C)	
2.	A · ~B	
3.	~(C ∨ D)	/∴ E · F
4.	A	2, Simp
5.	B ∨ C	1,4 MP
6.	~B	2, Simp
7.	C	5,6 DS
8.	~C · ~D	3, DeM
9.	~C	8, Simp
10.	C · ~C	7,9 Conj

75

Exercise 5-1

You should not have much trouble with these proofs. I will comment briefly on the choice of assumed premises in three of the problems. Although two assumed premises could be used in problem 3, the proof is simpler with only one, namely, A ⊃ B. The consequent of the conclusion follows from this assumption in one step by HS.

In constructing a proof for problem 5, it is best to use only one assumed premise, and, in fact, the proof is quite simple to construct without any assumptions. With one assumed premise, the proof looks like this:

```
→ 2.   A                    AP
  3.   C ∨ ~B               1, Add
  4.   ~B ∨ C               3, Comm
  5.   B ⊃ C                4, Impl
  6.   A ⊃ (B ⊃ C)          2-5 CP
```

With no assumptions, the proof would be as follows:

```
  2.   C ∨ ~B               1, Add
  3.   ~B ∨ C               2, Comm
  4.   B ⊃ C                3, Impl
  5.   (B ⊃ C) ∨ ~A         4, Add
  6.   ~A ∨ (B ⊃ C)         5, Comm
  7.   A ⊃ (B ⊃ C)          6, Impl
```

The problem which arises if you try to use two assumed premises in constructing the above proof is that you already have the consequent of the consequent of the conclusion on line 1 and need simply to rewrite it after making the two assumptions. Unfortunately, although any sentence clearly follows from itself, there is no valid argument form among the eighteen we have to work with which allows us simply to copy an existing line of a proof onto another line. We could get around this difficulty by simply using DN twice as follows:

```
    ┌──→2.  A                         AP
    │ ┌─→3.  B                         AP
    │ │  4.  ~~C                        1, DN
    │ │  5.  C _____  4, DN
    │ └─ 6.  B ⊃ C                      3-5 CP
    └─── 7.  A ⊃ (B ⊃ C)                2-6 CP
```

In problem 9, the proof is easiest to construct if you make use of both possible assumed premises, B and C.

Exercise 5-2

It is easiest to construct the proof for problem 1 if you work toward the contrapositive of the conclusion, that is, ~B ⊃ ~A, and assume its antecedent, namely, ~B.

You will need to use two assumed premises, K and M, to make problem 6 manageable.

Remember that problem 7 is not part of this exercise. Conditional proof does not make it much easier, and so working it here would essentially be returning to the skills required for the previous chapter and nothing more.

You will have to use Impl on the conclusion of problem 10 in order to turn it into a conditional sentence. After doing so, the choice of an assumed premise is straightforward.

Exercise 5-3

There are no really difficult problems here. Remember that any explicit contradiction will allow you to complete an indirect proof on the next line. All that you need is some sentence of the form $p \cdot {\sim}p$, and it doesn't matter whether the sentence represented by p is atomic or compound, part of the conclusion or premises, or a sentence that appears nowhere in the argument. If you are having trouble with this exercise, it probably means that you have forgotten some of the "strategy hints" or argument forms from the previous chapter. Go back and review them if you need to.

Exercise 5-4

With the exception of problem 1, all of the proofs in this exercise are both long and difficult if you do not use indirect proof. The message is pretty clear: conditional and indirect proof almost always make proofs shorter and easier to construct. If you use indirect proof throughout this exercise, only the final proof is very long, and none of the proofs should be very difficult for you.

Exercise 5-5

The last few problems in this exercise are quite long. There is nothing especially difficult about any of them however. I will work one problem from the middle of the exercise as an example for you, and try to put my thinking on paper.

(5) There is only one way to make the conclusion of this argument false, and that is to make B true. Once you do that, A must be false in order to make the first premise true. And once you have done that, C must be true or else the second premise would be false. So we can show that the argument is invalid by showing that if A were false and both B and C true, the argument would have true premises and a false conclusion, as the truth table analysis below demonstrates:

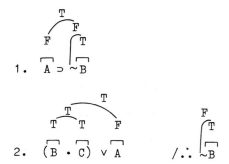

Exercise 5-6

As in the previous exercise, the problems at the end are quite long. I will do the third problem as an example.

(3) 1. $A \supset (B \lor C)$

2. $\sim(\sim A \lor C)$

3. $\sim B$ $/\therefore C$

Ignoring the conclusion, simply start to work on the premises using the "strategy hints" from the previous chapter until you can see how to reach an explicit contradiction. Remember that assumed premises are not allowed. You have to show that the premises alone are inconsistent, and you cannot do that by adding another sentence to them before you start. Here is the rest of problem 3:

4.	~~A • ~C	2, DeM
5.	~~A	4, Simp
6.	A	5, DN
7.	B ∨ C	1,6 MP
8.	~C	4, Simp
9.	~B • ~C	3,8 Conj
10.	~(B ∨ C)	9, DeM
11.	(B ∨ C) • ~(B ∨ C)	7,10 Conj

This could have been done in several ways. I purposely derived a contradiction which was neither an atomic sentence and its negation, nor the conclusion of the argument and its negation, just to reinforce the point made earlier in connection with indirect proof. When you need to derive an explicit contradiction, any sentence of the form p.~p will do the job.

Exercise 5-7

(3) I will do this problem as an example, and put my thinking on paper. Although it may not be apparent to you, C must be false. If it were true, then A would have to be true as well or the second premise would be false. But if C and A are both true, the first premise will be false. So C must be false, and D must be false as well to make the third premise true. Once C and D are false, all of the premises will be true regardless of the truth values you assign to A and B. So I will make them false as well, and demonstrate that all of the premises could be true by the truth table analysis below:

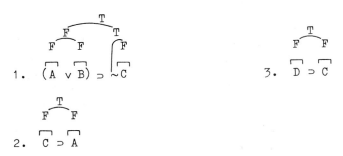

1. (A ∨ B) ⊃ ~C

2. C ⊃ A

3. D ⊃ C

Exercise 5-1   (Identifying Errors in Proofs of Validity)

Find and identify the errors in each of the following conditional or indirect proofs of validity.

(1) 1.　A ⊃ (~B · C)　　　　　p

2.　B ∨ D　　　　　p

3.　(C · D) ⊃ E　　　　　p

4.　A　　　　　AP

5.　C · D　　　　　AP

6.　E　　　　　3,5 MP

7.　A ⊃ E　　　　　4-6 CP

(2) 1.　F ⊃ (F ⊃ G)　　　　　p

2.　F　　　　　AP

3.　F ⊃ G　　　　　1,2 MP

(3) 1.　(M · N) ⊃ 0　　　　　p

2.　P ⊃ N　　　　　p

3.　P　　　　　AP

4.　M　　　　　AP

5.　N　　　　　2,3 MP

6.　M · N　　　　　4,5 Conj

7.　0　　　　　1,6 MP

8.　M ⊃ (P ⊃ 0)　　　　　3-7 CP

(4) 1. ~(A · B)   p

2. C ⊃ A   p

3. D ⊃ B   p

4. C · D   AP

5. ~A ∨ ~B   1, DeM

6. ~A ⊃ ~C   2, Contra

7. ~B ⊃ ~D   3, Contra

8. ~C ∨ ~D   5,6,7 CD

9. ~(C · D)   8, DeM

(5) 1. R ⊃ (S ⊃ T)   p

2. S ⊃ (T ⊃ W)   p

3. R   AP

4. S ⊃ T   1,3 MP

5. (S · T) ⊃ W   2, Exp

6. S   AP

7. T   4,6 MP

8. S · T   6,7 Conj

9. W   5,8 MP

10. S ⊃ W   6-9 CP

11. (S ⊃ W) ∨ ~R   10, Add

12. ~R ∨ (S ⊃ W)   11, Comm

13. R ⊃ (S ⊃ W)   12, Impl

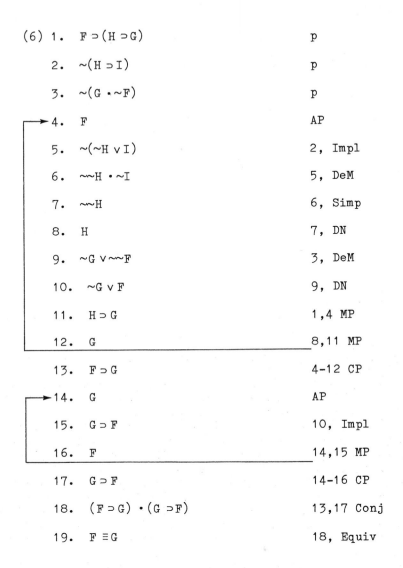

(6) 1. F ⊃ (H ⊃ G)   p

2. ~(H ⊃ I)   p

3. ~(G • ~F)   p

4. F   AP

5. ~(~H ∨ I)   2, Impl

6. ~~H • ~I   5, DeM

7. ~~H   6, Simp

8. H   7, DN

9. ~G ∨ ~~F   3, DeM

10. ~G ∨ F   9, DN

11. H ⊃ G   1,4 MP

12. G   8,11 MP

13. F ⊃ G   4-12 CP

14. G   AP

15. G ⊃ F   10, Impl

16. F   14,15 MP

17. G ⊃ F   14-16 CP

18. (F ⊃ G) • (G ⊃ F)   13,17 Conj

19. F ≡ G   18, Equiv

Exercise 5-2 (Conditional and Indirect Proof)

Prove the following arguments valid, using CP or IP.

(1) 1. M ⊃ N

2. O ⊃ P   /∴ (M • O) ⊃ (N • P)

(3) 1. (J ∨ K) ⊃ L

2. L ⊃ I   /∴ ~(~I • J)

(2) 1. G ⊃ (F ⊃ H)   ∴ F ⊃ (G ⊃ H)

(4) 1. F ⊃ G   /∴ (F ⊃ ~G) ⊃ ~(F • G)

(5) 1. H ⊃ ~G
   2. J ⊃ (K · H)   /∴ ~(G · J)

(6) 1. G ⊃ F   /∴ ~G ∨ (F ⊃ G)

(7) 1. (A ∨ B) ⊃ (C · D)
   2. (E ∨ F) ⊃ G /∴ A ⊃ [F ⊃ (D · G)]

(8) 1. (M ∨ N) ⊃ O
   2. ~(M ⊃ O)   /∴ P

(9) 1. R ⊃ [(S ∨ T) ⊃ U]
   2. U ⊃ W /∴ R ⊃ (S ⊃ W)

(10) 1. (N ∨ O) ⊃ M
   2. ~M   /∴ ~N

(11) 1. A ⊃ (B ∨ ~C)
   2. ~(A · ~C)
   3. ~B   /∴ ~A

(12) 1. N ⊃ O
   2. (O · P) ⊃ ~M /∴ M ⊃ (~N ∨ ~P)

(13) 1. (A ∨ B) ⊃ C
   2. D ⊃ A   /∴ ~C ⊃ ~D

(14) 1. M ⊃ (N ⊃ O)
   2. ~O ⊃ (M ⊃ N)
   3. ~M ⊃ O   /∴ O

(15) 1. R ⊃ (S ⊃ T)
   2. R ⊃ (S ⊃ W)
   3. R ⊃ S   /∴ R ⊃ (T · W)

(16) 1. ~(F ∨ G)
   2. H ⊃ (~G ⊃ F)   /∴ ~H

(17) 1. (F · G) ⊃ H
   2. ~(~G ∨ I)
   3. (H · ~I) ⊃ J   /∴ ~J ⊃ ~F

(18) 1. L ⊃ ~(M ∨ N)
   2. ~O ⊃ (~L ⊃ ~P)
   3. ~(P ⊃ Q)
   4. ~(L ⊃ M) ⊃ Q /∴ O

(19) 1. F ⊃ (G ≡ ~H)
   2. ~(I ∨ J)
   3. H ⊃ I
   4. G ⊃ ~F   /∴ F ⊃ J

(20) 1. Q   /∴ (R ∨ S) ≡ [(R ⊃ S) ⊃ S]

83

Exercise 5-3 (Concepts)

1. Must an invalid deductive argument:
    a. have true premises and a false conclusion?
    b. have consistent premises?
    c. have inconsistent premises?
    d. be sound?
    e. be unsound?

2. Can a deductive argument with consistent premises be:
    a. valid?
    b. invalid?
    c. sound?
    d. unsound?

3. Can a sound deductive argument:
    a. be valid?
    b. be invalid?
    c. have consistent premises?
    d. have inconsistent premises?
    e. have true premises?
    f. have false premises?

4. Must a valid deductive argument with consistent premises:
    a. have true premises?
    b. have a true conclusion?
    c. be sound?
    d. be unsound?
    e. have a true conclusion if its premises are true?
    f. have a true conclusion if it is sound?

5. Can a deductive argument with inconsistent premises be:
    a. valid?
    b. invalid?
    c. sound?
    d. unsound?

6. Can a deductive argument with consistent premises and a false conclusion:
    a. be valid?
    b. be invalid?
    c. have true premises?
    d. have false premises?
    e. be sound?
    f. be unsound?

Exercise 5-4 (Invalidity)

    Prove that the following arguments are invalid.

(1) 1. A ⊃ B

  2. C · (A ∨ B)   /∴ B ⊃ A

(2) 1. (F ∨ ~G) · H

  2. G ≡ H

  3. ~H ⊃ ~G   /∴ G ⊃ ~H

(3) 1. A ⊃ (B · C)

  2. B ∨ ~(C · A)

  3. ~A   /∴ ~B

(4) 1. H ⊃ G

  2. ~G ⊃ ~F

  3. ~[(G ⊃ H) ∨ F]   /∴ G ⊃ (H · F)

(5) 1. A ⊃ (B ⊃ C)

  2. ~(B · A)

  3. C · (~B ≡ ~A)   /∴ ~A ⊃ B

Exercise 5-5 (Premise Inconsistency)

  Show that the premises of the following arguments are inconsistent.

(1) 1. L · ~K

  2. J ∨ ~L

  3. J ⊃ K   /∴ M ⊃ K

(2) 1. W ⊃ T

  2. ~(S ⊃ T)

  3. W ∨ ~S   /∴ S ⊃ (T ⊃ W)

(3) 1. ~(~M ⊃ N)

  2. ~M ≡ (O · N)   /∴ O

(4) 1. ~R ⊃ S

  2. ~R ≡ T

  3. ~(T ⊃ S)   /∴ ~R ≡ (T ⊃ S)

(5) 1. ~(M · ~N)

  2. ~(P ∨ N)

  3. ~P ⊃ M   /∴ M ≡ O

Exercise 5-6 (Premise Consistency)

  Show that the premises of the following arguments are consistent.

(1) 1. M ⊃ N

2. ~N ⊃ ~O

3. ~M ∨ O   /∴ ~(M · O)

(2) 1. A ≡ (B · C)

2. B ⊃ C

3. ~(C ∨ A)   /∴ ~B

(3) 1. F ≡ G

2. H ∨ (G ⊃ F)

3. ~(G · H)   /∴ ~(F · G)

(4) 1. A ⊃ ~B

2. ~(B ∨ A) ∨ C

3. C ≡ ~B   /∴ A ⊃ ~C

(5) 1. ~(F · G)

2. ~G ≡ ~F

3. F ⊃ H   /∴ ~H

CHAPTER SIX

Predicate Logic--I

1   Translating Sentences in Predicate Logic

Here are some very important general rules of thumb to keep in mind
when translating sentences from English into the symbolic notation of
predicate logic.

(1) Universal quantifiers usually take " ⊃ " as the major connective
of the formula which follows them.

(2) Existential quantifiers usually take " · " as the major connective of the formula which follows them.

(3) Existential quantifiers almost never take " ⊃ " as the major
connective of the formula which follows them.

In addition to the 'grammar' rules introduced in the third chapter,
there is an additional rule in connection with translation in predicate
logic. Sentences in the symbolic notation of predicate logic cannot
contain free variables and cannot contain variables bound by more than
one quantifier. So it is important for you to be able to recognize the
difference between free and bound variables. A variable is free
whenever it is not bound by a quantifier. A quantifier binds every
variable of its kind (where kind is x, y, z, etc., the variable in terms
of which the quantifier is written) that occurs within its scope. And
the scope of a quantifier is the same as the scope of a negation sign
would be (that is, what it would negate) if it were in the same place as
the quantifier.

In general, sentences can be translated into the symbolic notation
of predicate logic in the following way:

First, identify the kind of thing which the sentence is about, and
put that in the second blank. For purposes of translation into symbolic
notation, sentences are not necessarily about their grammatical
subjects. They should be regarded as being about the first kind of
thing that the sentence talks about some or all of, that is, they are
about the first thing that will require a quantifier to translate. So,
for example, the sentence:

All trees are green.

is to be regarded as being about its grammatical subject, trees, because that is the first thing that the sentence talks about some or all of. However, the sentence:

George likes trees.

is not to be regarded as being about its grammatical subject, George. It is to be treated as a sentence about trees, because that is the first thing the sentence talks about some or all of. In this case the sentence is to be treated as being about all trees, and what it says about all things that are trees is that they have the property of being liked by George.

The next thing to do after filling in the second blank, is to ask yourself whether the sentence is about some (at least one) or all things of that kind. If some, put the existential quantifier, if all, put the universal quantifier, in the first blank. Remember that the quantifier variable must be the same as the variable you used in the second blank. So, for example, if the sentence were about trees and you put Tx in the second blank to indicate this, then the only universal quantifier which could be put into the first blank would be (x).

If you used the existential quantifier in the first blank, put the symbol for conjunction, " · ", in the third blank. If you used the universal quantifier in the first blank, put the symbol for material implication, " ⊃ ", in the third blank.

Finally, put in the fourth blank whatever the sentence predicates (says is true) of some or all things of the kind specified in the second blank. If the contents of either the second or the fourth blank are themselves compound, they will need to be enclosed in parentheses, brackets or braces to set them off from the rest of the sentence. Proper grouping requires that the connective in the third blank be the **major** connective of the entire formula following the quantifier in the first blank.

I will illustrate this general translation technique with the sentences I used as examples above, using natural abbreviations for the predicates and constant they contain.

All trees are green.

This sentence is about trees, so we would place the appropriate predicate in the second blank, as follows:

___ (___Tx___ ___ _____)

It is clearly about all rather than some trees, so we would next place the universal quantifier with the same variable that appears in the second blank into the first blank.

(x) (___Tx___ ___ _____)

Since the universal quantifier was used in the first blank, we must now place the symbol for material implication in the third blank.

$$(x) \ (\underline{\quad Tx \quad} \supset \underline{\qquad\qquad})$$

Finally, what the sentence says is true of all things that are trees is that they are green. So we should put that information into the fourth blank, again using the same variable that we have been using throughout the translation.

$$(x) \ (\underline{\quad Tx \quad} \supset \underline{\quad Gx \quad})$$

When we have completed the process above, we have the translation in symbolic notation of the sentence "All trees are green". The translation is $(x)(Tx \supset Gx)$. Now for the other sentence used as an example above:

George likes trees.

As the discussion above explained, this sentence is to be regarded as being about trees for purposes of translation. And since it is about all trees rather than some of them, the first three steps of the process will be identical to those above. The result would be:

$$(x) \ (\underline{\quad Tx \quad} \supset \underline{\qquad\qquad})$$

Now what the sentence says is true of all trees is that they are liked by George. So we should put that information into the fourth blank, again using the same variable that we have used in the other blanks.

$$(x) \ (\underline{\quad Tx \quad} \supset \underline{\quad Lgx \quad})$$

This means that the sentence "George likes trees" can be translated into the symbolic notation of predicate logic as $(x)(Tx \supset Lgx)$.

Relational predicates (predicates which are followed by more than one individual symbol and which express relations between or among individuals) are mentioned in this chapter of the text and used in some of the sentences in Exercise 6-1 and the examples preceding it. However, such predicates occur in the text only in sentences which can be translated without quantifiers, that is, sentences requiring only predicate and individual constants (and logical connectives in some cases) in the symbolic notation of predicate logic. I have already used a relational predicate with a quantifier in the second of the examples above. It would be good for you to become familiar with such sentences at this point. It will make the more difficult translations introduced in Chapter Eight a little easier to deal with when you get to them. Exercises 6-3 and 6-4 in this study guide will give you some practice with sentences involving a single quantifier and relational predicates. A few examples and their translations are provided below:

George doesn't like every tree. $\sim(x)(Tx \supset Lgx)$

There are some trees that George likes. $(\exists x)(Tx \cdot Lgx)$

There are no trees that George likes. $\sim(\exists x)(Tx \cdot Lgx)$ or
$(x)(Tx \supset \sim Lgx)$

The last example above brings up a point worth mentioning. As you should have gathered from the text by the time you completed this chapter, any sentence which can be translated by one kind of quantifier could also be translated using the other kind of quantifier. For most sentences there will be one quantifier which it is more natural to use, but for others the choice may be determined simply by the particular formulation you feel most comfortable using. And even a translation which is not the most 'natural' is still a perfectly good translation if it is logically equivalent to a correct translation of the sentence in question. At this point, however, it can be quite difficult for you to tell whether or not two sentences in symbolic notation are in fact equivalent, and this may make it difficult for you to know if your answers to the exercises match the answers in the back of the text or study guide when the quantifiers used are of different kinds. Here is what you will have to do in order to check.

Look at "Rule QN" inside the front cover of the text. It lists four equivalence formulas for changing sentences with one quantifier into sentences with the other quantifier. If doing so leaves the right quantifier at the beginning of the sentence, but a different formula following it, try using the equivalence argument forms from sentential logic on one of the two formulas. If it can be turned into the other by this means they are equivalent. If not, they are not.

There is a point made in the text concerning individual variables which is very important. The bound variables which occur in quantified sentences in predicate logic are not like individual constants at all in this respect. They have no identity whatsoever. Bound variables are simply placeholders in formulas which allow us to use the quantifiers. So the following sentences, for example:

$(x)(Tx \supset Gx)$ $(y)(Ty \supset Gy)$ $(z)(Tz \supset Gz)$ $(w)(Tw \supset Gw)$

are not just the same in structure, they are absolutely identical in meaning. Each of them says that everything which is T is also G, and it makes no difference whatsoever which variable we use to convey this information. If the predicates had the same meaning as those used in the examples discussed earlier, each of these formulations would translate as "All trees are green" with the particular variable used in each case making no contribution at all to the meaning of the sentence produced by using it.

The "domain of discourse" is the collection of things that sentences may be about. Normally we place no restrictions on this domain, and sentences may be about anything at all, anything in the universe. In such an unrestricted domain, if we want to say something about a certain group or kind of things, we have to build this into our translation. That is the point of the second blank in the general translation technique introduced above. So, for example, if I want to say that everyone is wonderful, I cannot just write (x)Wx, because that says that everything (sticks, stones, people and so on) is wonderful. I have to write (x)(Px ⊃ Wx), that is, I have to say about everything that, if it is a person (a one instead of a thing), then it is wonderful. In general, we narrow down the kinds of things we want to say something about by putting them in the antecedent of the conditional formula following a universal quantifier or in the first conjunct of the conjunction following an existential quantifier. To illustrate the latter, if I want to say that someone (that is, at least one 'one') is wonderful, I cannot just write (∃x)Wx, because that says that something (a stick, a stone, my pet guinea pig, who knows...) is wonderful. Instead I have to write (∃x)(Px · Wx), that is, I have to say that there is at least one thing which is both a person (a someone) and wonderful.

The reason for the above discussion is so that you are not misled by the examples in Section 5 of this chapter of the text. These translations assume an artificially restricted domain of discourse, and are correct only if we pretend that there is nothing in the universe except persons. The point of this restriction is to introduce you to multiple quantifiers of overlapping scope with as little additional complexity as possible. Section 3 of Chapter Eight of the text will cover this same material without artificial restriction. The important thing for you to keep in mind here is that you are not entitled to arbitrarily restrict the domain of discourse when translating in predicate logic. None of the **exercises** in either text or study guide places any restriction on the domain. And, unless clearly instructed to the contrary, you should always assume an unrestricted domain of discourse when translating sentences into or out of the symbolic notation of predicate logic.

The two pages which follow contain "translation hints" which should be quite helpful.

Translation Hints for Predicate Logic

1. Sentences which ascribe properties to individuals **by name** require no
quantifiers. They are translated by predicate constants and individual
constants (and logical connectives where needed). For example:

   (a) "a is F" = Fa (for example, "Art is fun to be with")

   (b) "a and b are F" = Fa · Fb (for example, "Art and Betsy are fun
to be with")

   (c) "a stands in the relation F to b" = Fab (for example, "Art is
fatter than Betsy")

2. Sentences which ascribe properties to every individual or to every
individual of a specified kind are translated using the universal
quantifier. Such sentences frequently begin with "all", "every" or
"any". Examples of such sentences follow:

   (a) "All F's are G" = (x)(Fx ⊃ Gx) (for example, "All fools are
gullible")

   (b) "Every F is G" = (x)(Fx ⊃ Gx) (for example, "Every fool is
gullible")

   (c) "Any F is G" = (x)(Fx ⊃ Gx) (for example, "Any fool is
gullible")

   (d) "F's are G" = (x)(Fx ⊃ Gx) (for example, "Fools are gullible")

3. Sentences which ascribe properties to some (but not all) individuals
or to some individuals of a specified kind are translated using the
existential quantifier. Such sentences frequently begin with "some" or
"there is/are". Examples of such sentences follow:

   (a) "Some F's are G" = (∃x)(Fx · Gx) (for example, "Some fools are
gullible")

   (b) "There are F's that are G" = (∃x)(Fx · Gx) (for example, "There
are fools that are
gullible")

   (c) "There are G F's" = (∃x)(Fx · Gx) (for example, "There are
gullible fools")

4. The following negative constructions can be translated by either one
of the pair of translations indicated. In each case I have given the
translation which seems to me to be the more natural of the two first.

(a) "Not all F's are G" = $\sim(x)(Fx \supset Gx)$ or $(\exists x)(Fx \cdot \sim Gx)$

(b) "Not every F is G" = $\sim(x)(Fx \supset Gx)$ or $(\exists x)(Fx \cdot \sim Gx)$

(c) "No F's are G" = $\sim(\exists x)(Fx \cdot Gx)$ or $(x)(Fx \supset \sim Gx)$

(d) "None of the F's are G" = $\sim(\exists x)(Fx \cdot Gx)$ or $(x)(Fx \supset \sim Gx)$

(e) "Nothing that is F is G" = $\sim(\exists x)(Fx \cdot Gx)$ or $(x)(Fx \supset \sim Gx)$

(f) "There are not any F's that are G" = $\sim(\exists x)(Fx \cdot Gx)$ or $(x)(Fx \supset \sim Gx)$

5. The English word "any" is ambiguous in terms of the quantity of things it picks out. It can require either the universal or the existential quantifier as its translation. In general, you can tell which is required in the following way. If the word "any" is in the subject position (is the grammatical subject) of its sentence or clause, it requires the universal quantifier. If it is in the object position (is the grammatical object) of its sentence or clause, it requires the existential quantifier. If you want another way to check that you have chosen the correct quantifier, you can do the following. Try substituting "every" for "any" in the English sentence, and then try substituting "even one" for "any" in the same sentence. If the former substitution seems to capture the meaning better, use the universal quantifier. If the latter, use the existential quantifier.

6. Whenever possible, break complex sentences down into their simpler parts and translate the parts individually.

7. Try transforming the English equivalents of the quantifiers ("some", "all", "every" and so on) into the following awkward constructions before translating:

For the words which require the universal quantifier, use: "Everything (in the universe) is such that..."

For the words which require the universal quantifier, use: "There is at least one thing (in the universe) which is such that..."

8. To check your translations into symbolic notation, try to translate your sentences from symbols back into English and see if you get a sentence which is equivalent in meaning or truth conditions to the sentence with which you started.

2 Expansions of Quantified Sentences

Expansions of quantified sentences are used in this chapter of the text to help you understand what information certain sentences convey in terms of what they would mean in a universe consisting of only two or three individuals where no quantifiers would be required. In Chapter Eight you will find that producing expansions allows us to demonstrate the invalidity of arguments and the consistency of premises in predicate logic.

The examples which precede Exercises 6-6 and 6-10, along with the discussions they contain, may be sufficient to enable you to construct expansions of such sentences on your own with little or no difficulty. In the event that some of these expansions remain very difficult for you to come up with, however, I will give you a mechanical technique for expanding all such quantified sentences into a universe consisting of two individuals, a and b, below.

(1) Sentences of the form (x)(...x...) become:

(...a...) · (...b...)

where the formulas inside the parentheses are identical to (...x...) except for having a and b respectively at every place that (...x...) has x.

So, for example, (x)[(Fx · Gx) ⊃Hx] becomes:

[(Fa · Ga) ⊃Ha] · [(Fb · Gb) ⊃Hb]

(2) Sentences of the form (∃x)(...x...) become:

(...a...) ∨ (...b...)

where the formulas inside the parentheses are identical to (...x...) except for having a and b respectively at every place that (...x...) has x.

So, for example, (∃x)(Fx · ~Gx) becomes:

(Fa · ~Ga) ∨ (Fb · ~Gb)

(3) Sentences of the form (x)(y)(...x,y...) become:

$$
\overset{1}{[(...a,a...)} \cdot \overset{2}{(...a,b...)]} \cdot \overset{3}{[(...b,a...)} \cdot \overset{4}{(...b,b...)]}
$$

Sentences of the form $(\exists x)(\exists y)(\ldots x,y\ldots)$ become:

$$\underbrace{[(\ldots a,a\ldots)}_{1} \vee \underbrace{(\ldots a,b\ldots)]}_{2} \vee [\underbrace{(\ldots b,a\ldots)}_{3} \vee \underbrace{(\ldots b,b\ldots)}_{4}]$$

Sentences of the form $(x)(\exists y)(\ldots x,y\ldots)$ become:

$$\underbrace{[(\ldots a,a\ldots)}_{1} \vee \underbrace{(\ldots a,b\ldots)]}_{2} \cdot [\underbrace{(\ldots b,a\ldots)}_{3} \vee \underbrace{(\ldots b,b\ldots)}_{4}]$$

Sentences of the form $(\exists x)(y)(\ldots s,y\ldots)$ become:

$$\underbrace{[(\ldots a,a\ldots)}_{1} \cdot \underbrace{(\ldots a,b\ldots)]}_{2} \vee [\underbrace{(\ldots b,a\ldots)}_{3} \cdot \underbrace{(\ldots b,b\ldots)}_{4}]$$

where the formulas in each of the numbered parentheses are identical to $(\ldots x,y\ldots)$ except for having:

  i. a where $(\ldots x,y\ldots)$ has x and a where $(\ldots x,y\ldots)$ has y in the first parentheses,

  ii. a where $(\ldots x,y\ldots)$ has x and b where $(\ldots x,y\ldots)$ has y in the second parentheses,

  iii. b where $(\ldots x,y\ldots)$ has x and a where $(\ldots x,y\ldots)$ has y in the third parentheses, and

  iv. b where $(\ldots x,y\ldots)$ has x and b where $(\ldots x,y\ldots)$ has y in the fourth parentheses.

So, for example, $(x)(y)Gxy$ becomes:

  $(Gaa \cdot Gab) \cdot (Gba \cdot Gbb)$

and $(\exists x)(\exists y)Gxy$ becomes:

  $(Gaa \vee Gab) \vee (Gba \vee Gbb)$

and $(x)(\exists y)Gxy$ becomes:

  $(Gaa \vee Gab) \cdot (Gba \vee Gbb)$

and $(\exists x)(y)Gxy$ becomes:

  $(Gaa \cdot Gab) \vee (Gba \cdot Gbb)$

95

You need to be very careful about how you interpret all of the recipes for constructing expansions on the preceding pages. In the case of sentences with a single quantifier, (1) and (2) above, the choice of x for the variable in terms of which the recipes were written is entirely arbitrary. To keep from being misled you should read "the variable in terms of which the quantifier and sentence are written" where I have written x in (1) and (2) above. In the case of sentences with multiple quantifiers, (3) above, the choice of x first and y second was also entirely arbitrary. To keep from being misled, you should read "first quantifier variable" (that is, the variable with which the first quantifier of the sentence is written) where I have written x and "second quantifier variable" where I have written y. So, for example, in the parentheses numbered 2 in the expansions of all of the two-quantifier sentences in (3) above, you are really substituting a for the first quantifier variable (whatever it may be, x, y, z, etc., and wherever it may occur in the formula following the quantifiers), and b for the second quantifier variable. You cannot just blindly substitute a for x and b for y regardless of the variables in terms of which the quantifiers are written. And you cannot just blindly produce aa, ab, ba, and bb following the predicates in the expansion regardless of the order in which the quantifier variables appear after the predicates in the quantified sentence. Here are some examples which illustrate the points just made.

Sentence	Expansion
$(z)[(Fz \cdot Gz) \supset Hz]$	$[(Fa \cdot Ga) \supset Ha] \cdot [(Fb \cdot Gb) \supset Hb]$
$(\exists w)(Fw \cdot {\sim}Gw)$	$(Fa \cdot {\sim}Ga) \vee (Fb \cdot {\sim}Gb)$
$(\exists y)(x)Gyx$	$(Gaa \cdot Gab) \vee (Gba \cdot Gbb)$
$(\exists x)(y)Gyx$	$(Gaa \cdot Gba) \vee (Gab \cdot Gbb)$
$(\exists y)(x)Gxy$	$(Gaa \cdot Gba) \vee (Gab \cdot Gbb)$

3 Proving Validity

Since the discussion of proofs of validity in predicate logic will be confined to the next two chapters of this study guide, the material in Section 4 of this chapter of the text will not be covered here.

Discussion of Exercises from Text

Exercise 6-1

I have two comments to make concerning this exercise. The first is that it contains an extraordinary number of truth-functionally meaningless introductory words and phrases, such as "In fact", "But", "So, obviously", "Nevertheless" and so on. Just ignore all of them when you translate these sentences. The second comment I have is that none of these sentences requires a quantifier in its translation. They are all to be tranlated using predicate and individual constants, along with the logical connectives where needed. This should present no problem for you now. But by the time you reach the end of this chapter or Section 3 of Chapter Eight of the text, you may be so concerned with quantifiers that you could forget (at exam time, for example) that sentences like these cannot be translated with quantifiers. Try to remember it.

Exercise 6-2

This exercise should give you no trouble at all. If you are having any difficulty with it, refer back to the discussion of quantifier scope in the text and study guide.

Exercise 6-3

I will translate two of these for you, and try to put my thinking down on paper for you.

5. This sentence is about natural events, and about all rather than some of them. So the translation technique introduced above would give us this as the outcome of the first three steps for translating this sentence:

$$(x)[(Nx \cdot Ex) \supset \quad]$$

What the sentence says is true of all natural events is that they have causes. Putting this information in as the consequent of the conditional formula above completes the translation as follows:

$$(x)[(Nx \cdot Ex) \supset Cx]$$

7. This sentence is about no unnatural events. Using the construction suggested in the "tranlation hints" for translating sentences which begin with "No", gives us:

$$\sim(\exists x)\big[(\sim Nx \cdot Ex) \cdot \quad \big]$$

as the translation of the subject of the sentence with quantifier
and major connective. Now what the sentence says is true of no
unnatural events is that they have causes. Putting this in as the
second conjunct of the formula above completes the translation as
follows:

$$\sim(\exists x)\big[(\sim Nx \cdot Ex) \cdot Cx\big]$$

Of course, at this point in the text, only the universal quantifier
has been introduced, so if you have not looked ahead or worked with
the "translation hints" in this study guide, you could not have
translated the sentence as I did above. Here is how to think about
the sentence so as to come up with the correct translation using
the universal quantifier. If no unnatural events have causes,
then all unnatural events must fail to have causes. That is, all
unnatural events must be uncaused, and so the sentence can be translated as though it were about all unnatural events:

$$(x)\big[(\sim Nx \cdot Ex) \supset \quad \big]$$

And since what it says is true of all such events is that they are
not caused, the complete translation is as follows:

$$(x)\big[(\sim Nx \cdot Ex) \supset \sim Cx\big]$$

Exercise 6-4

As with the previous exercise, I will translate two of these
sentences for you and try to put my thinking down on paper as I do so.

5. This sentence is composed of two separate smaller sentences, and
these must be translated individually as the "translation hints"
from this chapter indicate. Rewriting the sentence slightly in
English makes this apparent:

If all logic students are logical, then no logic student is popular.

The first sentence is about all logic students, and since it says of
them that they are all logical, it can be translated as:

$$(x)(Sx \supset Lx)$$

The second sentence is about no logic students. If we use the
existential quantifier as in the discussion of the previous exercise, above, the translation would be:

$$\sim(\exists x)(Sx \cdot Px)$$

If we use the universal quantifier as the text assumes for this exercise, the translation would follow from the same line of thought we followed in translating sentence 7 from Exercise 6-3. The resulting translation would be:

$$(x)(Sx \supset \sim Px)$$

Now the whole sentence is a conditional, whose antecedent and consequent we have just translated. Depending upon the translation of the consequent sentence, the result is either:

$$(x)(Sx \supset Lx) \supset \sim(\exists x)(Sx \cdot Px) \text{ or}$$

$$(x)(Sx \supset Lx) \supset (x)(Sx \supset \sim Px)$$

7. Rewriting this sentence in English gives us:

It is false that all the unpopular are illogical.

This will translate as the negation of the universally quantified sentence which says of all the unpopular that they are not logical, and so can be translated as follows:

$$\sim(x)(\sim Px \supset \sim Lx)$$

Exercise 6-5

The "translation hints" in this chapter of the study guide should be sufficient to enable you to translate any of these sentences into symbolic notation. If you have trouble with any of them, refer to the discussion of translation at the beginning of this chapter of the study guide.

Exercise 6-6

The technique for expanding quantified sentences introduced in this chapter of the study guide will give you the expansions for any of these sentences.

Exercise 6-7

It should not be difficult for you to get these sentences into some sort of English. What you need to pay special attention to, however, is getting them into colloquial or natural sounding English sentences. If you really understand the truth conditions of the sentences in symbols, you should have no trouble expressing them in the natural way a typical speaker of English would do so. For example, if you translate sentences 3 and 5 as follows:

3. It is false that some TV newscaster is a political expert.

5. It is false that all things are such that if they are TV news-
    casters, then they are political experts.

you may, in fact, have captured the truth conditions of those sentences. But one would have to assume that you did not understand those truth conditions. If you had, you would have expressed them much more natu- rally as do the following translations:

3. No TV newscaster is a political expert.

5. Not every TV newscaster is a political expert.

Exercise 6-8

Some of these sentences may involve a few more predicates than those of previous exercises in this chapter, but none of these are any more difficult to translate than the sentences from Exercises 6-4 and 6-5. Refer to the "translation hints" if you have any trouble with them.

Exercise 6-9

Since the discussion of proofs of validity in predicate logic will be confined to the next two chapters of this study guide, there is no discussion of this exercise. You might want to look ahead to the first few pages of the next chapter of the study guide if you do not understand exactly what is going on either in this exercise or in the discussion preceding it.

Exercise 6-10

I will translate sentences 4 and 8 for you, even though answers are available in the back of the text, because I want to comment on the important difference between them.

4. $(x)(\exists y)Sxy$

8. $(\exists y)(x)Sxy$

I have used x and y in the reverse of the order in which they appear in the answer in the text for sentence 8 so that it would be clear just what the difference between these two sentences is. The only difference between them is the order of the quantifiers. By picking out the something first, sentence 8 says that there is some (one) thing in the universe such that everything is smaller than it. Roughly speaking, that means there is a largest thing in the universe.

On the other hand, by picking out everything first, sentence 4 says of every individual thing in the universe that it is smaller than something or other; but the something or other need not be the same thing in each case (that is the point of the "or other" in the text). So sentence 4 does not say, even roughly, that there is a largest thing in the universe. In fact it rules that out by putting every single thing in the universe on the smaller end of a size relationship with something or other.

Exercise 6-1 (Translation in Predicate Logic)

Ax = "x is an alien"   Cxy = "x commands y"
Ex = "x is emotional"   Fxy = "x is fond of y"
Fx = "x is from the Federation" Lxy = "x lands on y"
Hx = "x is hostile"
Kx = "x is a Klingon"   e = "the Enterprise"
Px = "x is a planet"   k = "Kirk"
Sx = "x is a starship"   m = "McCoy"
Vx = "x is a Vulcan"   s = "Spock"

Symbolize the following sentences, using the predicate and
individual constants above.

1. The Enterprise is a Federation starship.

2. Spock is a Vulcan, not a Klingon.

3. The Enterprise is not an alien starship.

4. Kirk, McCoy and Spock are from the Federation.

5. Neither Kirk nor McCoy is an alien.

6. Kirk is neither a Vulcan nor a Klingon.

7. Kirk and Spock are fond of each other.

8. Kirk and Spock are fond of each other and of the Enterprise.

9. Kirk is fond of both Spock and McCoy, and they are fond of him as
    well.

10. Neither Spock nor McCoy command the Enterprise, but Kirk does.

Exercise 6-2 (Translation in Predicate Logic)

Translate the following sentences into English, being as
colloquial as possible. The constants have the same meanings
as in Exercise 6-1 above.

1. Ek · Em

2. Fms · ~Es

3. ~(Es ∨ As)

4. Cse • ~Cme

5. (Fe • Se) • Cke

6. (~Vk • ~Vm) • Vs

7. ~(Csm ∨ Cms)

8. ~[(Hk • Ak) ∨ (Hm • Am)]

9. Cme ⊃ Es

10. {(Fks • Fkm) • [(Fmk • Fms) • (Fsk • Fsm)]} • [(Fke • Fse) • Fme]

Exercise 6-3 (Translation in Predicate Logic)

Bx = "x is boring"	Kxy = "x knows y"
Cx = "x is a course"	Pxy = "x passes y"
Dx = "x is difficult"	Txy = "x takes y"
Ex = "x is an exam"	
Fx = "x is friendly"	Lxyz = "x learns y from z"
Ix = "x is interesting"	
Sx = "x is a student"	c = "Christina"
	g = "George"
	j = "John"
	m = "Mary"

Symbolize the following sentences, using the predicate and individual constants above.

1. Students are friendly.

2. Boring courses are not interesting.

3. Some difficult courses are interesting.

4. There are interesting courses which are not difficult.

5. Not every exam is difficult.

6. No students are both interesting and boring.

7. No interesting courses are boring.

8. George knows some boring students.

9. John has not taken any difficult courses.

10. Mary has passed every exam she has taken.

11. George has not learned anything from himself.

12. Every student knows George.

13. John knows some friendly students, but he doesn't know Christina.

14. Some students know John but do not know Mary.

15. George learned something from Christina.

16. George doesn't know everything.

17. George doesn't know every student.

18. John doesn't pass every course he takes.

19. John learned everything he knows from Mary.

20. George learned everything John knows from him.

Exercise 6-4 (Translation in Predicate Logic)

Translate the following sentences into English, being as colloquial as possible. The constants have the same meanings as in Exercise 6-3 above.

1. (x)(Ex ⊃ Dx)

2. (x)[(Cx • Dx) ⊃~Bx]

3. (∃y)(Cy • ~Iy)

4. (∃x)[(Cx • Dx) • ~Ix]

5. ~(x)[Cx ⊃ (Dx ∨ Bx)]

6. (∃x)[Cx • ~(Ix ∨ Dx)]

7. ~(y)(Sy ⊃ Fy)

8. ~(∃y)(Cy • Dy)

9. (y)[(Iy • Cy) ⊃~Tgy]

10. (x)[(Sx • Ix) ⊃~Kjx]

11. (∃x)(Sx • Kxg)

12. (∃y)[(Cy • By) • Tgy]

13. ~(x)Ljxj

14. (∃x)Ljxm

15. (∃x)[(Ex • Tjx) • Pjx]

16. ~(x)[(Ex • Tjx) ⊃ Pjx]

17. (x)[(Cx • Tmx) ⊃ Tjx]

18. ~(x)[(Cx • Pmx) ⊃ Pjx]

19. ~(∃x)[(Ex • Pjx) • ~Pmx]

20. (x)(Kgx ⊃ Lgxc)

Exercise 6-5 (Expanding Quantified Sentences)

Construct expansions in a two-individual universe of discourse for the following sentences.

1. $(\exists x)Ax$

2. $(\exists x)\sim Bx$

3. $(y)(Ay \supset By)$

4. $(\exists x)(Fx \cdot \sim Hx)$

5. $(x)[(Ax \cdot Bx) \supset Cx]$

6. $(\exists y)\sim(Fy \vee Gy)$

7. $(x)[(Ax \cdot Bx) \supset Cxx]$

8. $(\exists y)(May \cdot Mby)$

9. $(x)(Fxx \supset Gxx)$

10. $(x)(y)Myx$

11. $(\exists x)(\exists y)Gxy$

12. $(\exists y)(x)Mxy$

13. $(\exists x)(y)(Fy \supset Gyx)$

14. $(x)(\exists y)(Fx \supset Gxy)$

15. $(\exists y)(x)Mxay$

16. $(y)(\exists x)Mxay$

CHAPTER SEVEN

Predicate Logic--II

1 Proofs in Predicate Logic without Quantifier Negation

The first part of this chapter of the text formulates precisely the four implicational quantifier rules for constructing proofs of validity in predicate logic, and provides examples and instructions for using them.

The formulation of the first four quantifier rules on p.123 (and on the right-hand page inside the front cover of the text) may seem somewhat confusing to you. There are two things which frequently lead to difficulty in understanding these rules. The first is the notation in which they are written, that is, the use of u, w, (...u...) and (...w...). The second source of difficulty is that the restrictions on the use of these rules are not of a single kind or collected in a single place in the formulation of them. I will try to add to the discussion in the text on both these points in case they are giving you any problems in understanding what the rules are or what they really mean in practice.

The point of the rules, that is, the reason for having them, is clear. In order to use the implicational argument forms of sentential logic on the information contained within quantified premises, we need to be able to remove the quantifiers. And in order to reach a quantified conclusion after doing so, we must be able to, in some sense, 'put the quantifiers back on'. These quantifier rules tell us when and how to do so.

In the formulation of the rules, u and w are not ordinary individual variables. You might think of them as super-variables. Ordinary variables stand for individual constants only. These super-variables stand for individual constants and (ordinary) individual variables as well. So when you see u, for example, just read "any individual constant or variable u", and do the same for w. The expression (...u...) stands for any formula which contains the individual constant or variable for which the super-variable u stands. So, for example, the following formulas:

Fa • Gx
(Ǝx)Hax
(x)(y)[(Mx • Ny) ⊃ Oxay]
Fa
(Fa • Ga) ⊃ Ha

could all be represented by (...u...) where u stands for the individual constant a. Or they could all be represented by (...w...) where w

stands for the individual constant a. The first formula above could
also be represented by (...u...) where u stands for the individual
variable x. The second formula could be represented by (∃u)(...u...)
where u stands for the individual variable x. The third formula could
be represented by (u)(...u...) where u stands for the individual
variable x. However, for purposes of Rule UI or Rule UG, the third
formula could not be represented by (u)(...u...) or (w)(...w...) where u
and w stand for the individual variable y because the (y) quantifier and
the formula following it are not a complete line, but are instead part
of a larger sentence; and all of the first four quantifier rules can be
used only on complete lines of a proof because they are implicational
rather than equivalence argument forms.

This brings us to the restrictions on the use of these quantifier
rules. One kind of restriction which applies to all of them is that
just mentioned above. All of these are implicational argument forms and
can only be used on complete lines of a proof. This means that the only
quantifiers you can ever add to or remove from lines of a proof are
quantifiers which appear at the very beginning of the line (without
other quantifiers or negation signs or anything else in front of them)
and whose scope includes everything following them on the line. The
remaining restrictions on the use of these rules are contained in the
brief paragraph which precedes them (the one which begins "First, let u
and w ...") and in the numbered items following the individual rules. I
will suggest a slightly different way to divide these than is used in
the text, and then try to make it a little easier for you to understand
what some of the more mysterious looking restrictions actually mean.

If you separate the fourth of the numbered restrictions following
Rule UG and the only numbered restriction following Rule EG from the
rest of the numbered restrictions on the four quantifier rules, the
result is as follows. The remaining numbered restrictions are quite
clear and easy to understand from the examples in the text which
illustrate their violation in various contexts. And those two numbered
restrictions which you have removed, together with the little paragraph
preceding the rules, represent general restrictions on the use of the
four quantifier rules which can be put into fairly plain English as
follows.

(1) Whenever you remove a quantifier, you must actually free by so
    doing all symbols and only those symbols which had been bound
    by the quantifier you are removing. The resulting line must be
    identical to the line from which the quantifier is removed
    except that the quantifier is gone and a single kind of free
    symbol occurs throughout the new line at each point where the
    old line had contained a symbol bound by that quantifier.

(2) Whenever you add a quantifier, only one kind of previously free
    symbol must become bound by so doing. If a universal quanti-
    fier is added, every previously free symbol of that same kind
    must become bound by it. If an existential quantifier is
    added, at least one of that kind of previously free symbol must
    become bound by it. No changes can be made to the line to

which either quantifier is added other than the addition of the quantifier and the changing of free symbols to symbols bound by that quantifier.

The following examples illustrate the typical ways in which the general restrictions (1) and (2) above can be violated in practice.

．
．
．

m. $(\exists x)(y)(Fx \cdot Gxy)$

n. $(y)(Fy \cdot Gyy)$ m, EI   No symbol was actually freed by removing the quantifier.

．
．
．

m. $(x)(y)(Fx \supset Gxy)$

n. $(y)(Fy \supset Gyy)$ m, UI   No symbol was actually freed by removing the quantifier.

．
．
．

m. $(\exists x)[Fx \cdot (y)Gxy]$

n. $Fy \cdot (y)Gyy$ m, EI   Not every symbol previously bound by the quantifier was actually freed by removing it.

．
．
．

m. $(y)[Fy \supset (\exists x)Gyx]$

n. $Fx \supset (\exists x)Gxx$ m, UI   Not every symbol previously bound by the quantifier was actually freed by removing it.

．
．
．

m. $(x)(Fx \supset Gx)$

n. $Fx \supset Gy$ m, UI   Substitution was not systematic. Two different kinds of free symbols resulted.

.
.
.

m. $(\exists x)(Fx \cdot \sim Gx)$

n. $Fy \cdot \sim Gz$ m, EI   Substitution was not sys-
                                                tematic. Two different kinds
                                                of free symbols resulted.

.
.
.

m. $(x)(Fx \supset Gx)$

n. $(y)(Fy \supset Gy)$ m, UG   The symbol which has been
                                                bound by the quantifier was
                                                not previously free, and the
                                                quantifier from the previous
                                                line has disappeared.

.
.
.

m. $(\exists y)Fyy$

n. $(\exists x)(\exists y)Fxy$ m, EG   The symbol which has been
                                                bound by the quantifier was
                                                not previously free.

.
.
.

m. $Fx \supset Gx$

n. $(y)(Fx \supset Gy)$ m, UG   Not every free symbol of the
                                                kind which was free and has
                                                become bound has in fact
                                                become bound.

.
.
.

m. $Fx \supset Gy$

n. $(x)(Fx \supset Gx)$ m, UG   The quantifier added binds
                                                previously free symbols of
                                                two different kinds.

.
.
.

m. $Fa \cdot Gb$

n. (∃x)(Fx · Gx)   m, EG   The quantifier added binds
                                                  previously free symbols of
                                                  two different kinds.

The preceding discussion has the following result. All you need to
do in order to understand all of the restrictions which could apply to
the use of the first four quantifier rules is the following:

1. Remember that these rules are implicational argument forms and
can only be used on complete lines of a proof.

2. Remember the general restrictions (1) and (2) above which apply
to the use of these rules.

3. Remember the two specific restrictions which apply to Rule EI and
the three (first three of the four in the text) specific restrictions
which apply to Rule UG.

In practice, the task is even easier than this. The two specific
restrictions which you will find yourself most often tempted to violate
are the second restriction on Rule EI and the second restriction on Rule
UG. If you make a special effort to keep these in mind and to remember
that all four of these rules can be used only on complete lines of a
proof, correct use of these quantifier rules should come fairly
naturally to you.

2 Conditional Proof in Predicate Logic

Conditional proof may be used in predicate logic on two different
sorts of conclusions, those which have two separate sentences (which may
or may not contain quantifiers) joined by " ⊃ ", and those which consist
of a single quantified sentence with a conditional formula following the
quantifier. Examples of these two kinds of conclusions, respectively,
are:

(1) (x)(Fx ⊃ Gx) ⊃ Ha, and

(2) (x)[(Fx · Gx) ⊃ Hx]

For the first sort of conclusion, the appropriate assumed premise
is the entire antecedent of the conclusion, quantifier and all. So for
(1) above we would assume (x)(Fx ⊃ Gx) and then try to derive Ha. After
deriving Ha we would write (x)(Fx ⊃ Gx) ⊃ Ha on the following line and
justify it by CP.

For the second sort of conclusion, the appropriate assumed premise
is the antecedent of the formula following the quantifier without any
quantifier in the assumed premise. So for (2) above we would assume
Fx · Gx (or Fy · Gy, Fz · Gz, etc.) and then try to derive Hx (or Hy, Hz,
etc.). We would then write the entire conditional formula on the next

line, justifying it by CP. On the following line of the proof we could
write the conclusion of the argument and justify it by UG, assuming we
had chosen a variable which did not force us to violate any of the
restrictions on UG at this point.

3 Proofs Involving Quantifier Negation

There are no special difficulties connected with the use of Rule
QN. It is important to remember that it is an equivalence argument form
and can be used on parts of lines as well as on complete lines of a
proof. And each of the four formulas under the rule can be used in
either direction. This gives you, in effect, eight different ways in
which quantifier kinds can be changed by Rule QN. So, for example, the
following move is perfectly legitimate:

.
.
.

m. $(\exists x)(y)\sim Fxy$

n. $(\exists x)\sim(\exists y)Fxy$ m, QN

because Rule QN is an equivalence argument form and can be used on the
part of line m following the first quantifier. And the following pair
of steps is unnecessary:

.
.
.

m. $\sim(\exists x)\sim Fx$

n. $(x)\sim\sim Fx$ m, QN

o. $(x)Fx$ n, DN

because another one of the eight equivalence formulas would have taken
you directly from line m to line o in one step by QN.

Rule QN makes it possible to use the technique of indirect proof on
arguments in predicate logic. This technique is at least as useful here
as it was in sentential logic, if not more so. There will be times when
an indirect proof makes it much easier for you to avoid violations of
the restrictions on the first four quantifier rules. Indirect proof is
also a very important last resort to keep in mind whenever you are
having serious problems with a proof in predicate logic.

Although Rule QN is not especially difficult to master, it does
allow you to construct proofs of validity for a much wider range of
arguments in predicate logic than you encountered in the first part of
this chapter. Some of these arguments are very difficult to prove
valid, even with Rule QN and the rest of the valid argument forms of

sentential and predicate logic. Do not let very difficult proofs tempt
you to violate the restrictions on the use of the first four quantifier
rules.

The following page contains "strategy hints" for constructing
proofs of validity in predicate logic.

Strategy Hints for Proofs in Predicate Logic

1. If you cannot see immediately how to come up with a proof, try rewriting the entire argument using only the predicate constants and connectives, that is, dropping all the quantifiers, variables and individual constants from the premises and conclusion. Looking at the argument in this form will usually show you the sentential logic required to get from premises to conclusion. Then all you have to do is figure out how to use the quantifier rules so that the necessary sentential logic moves become possible.

2. UI, EI, UG and EG are implicational argument forms. Never use them on parts of lines in a proof.

3. Formulas following quantifiers are to be regarded as parts of lines only. The first four quantifier rules cannot be used on them until the initial quantifiers have been removed by UI and/or EI. Never use any of the implicational argument forms of sentential logic on such formulas either without first removing the quantifiers.

4. QN and the equivalence argument forms of sentential logic can be used on formulas following quantifiers without first removing any of the quantifiers. Do not remove quantifiers unnecessarily, that is, when the use of equivalence argument forms alone will enable you to complete a proof.

5. When an argument has both universally and existentially quantified premises which will have to be instantiated in the proof, always instantiate the existentially quantified premises first. In other words, always use EI before UI when possible. This will allow you to use the same variable to instantiate both an existentially quantified premise and any universally quantified premises without violating restrictions on the use of the quantifier rules. In this way the information in the various premises can be brought together, and this is usually necessary in order to reach the conclusion of an argument.

6. Whenever the conclusion of an argument is a negated quantified sentence (a sentence beginning with ~($\exists$u) or ~(u) for some variable u), try using indirect proof. The assumed premise will then begin with a doubly negated existential or universal quantifier, which can be instantiated after the double negation is dropped.

7. Whenever the conclusion of an argument is an existentially quantified sentence and you cannot see how to construct the proof directly, try using indirect proof. After using QN on the assumed premise, you will be left with a universally quantified sentence. And those are the easiest quantified sentences to work with in a proof because they can be instantiated with any individual symbol, constant or variable.

Discussion of Exercises from Text

Exercise 7-1

This exercise should not be difficult for you. I will provide below a slightly rewritten version of the answers in the back of the text which brings them into line with the restrictions on the use of the quantifier rules as I have presented them in this chapter of the study guide.

(2) 1. The inference to line 4 is invalid because x is free in line 2, which was obtained by EI.

2. The inference to line 6 is invalid because there has been a change made other than that required to bind one or more of the free y's in line 5 by the new quantifier.

(4) 1. The inference to line 3 is invalid because nothing has been freed by removing the quantifier.

2. The inference to line 5 is invalid because line 2 does not contain the antecedent of the conditional formula on line 4.

3. The inference to line 8 is invalid because two different kinds of free symbols have been bound by the added quantifier.

4. The inference to line 9 is invalid because line 9 does not contain the conjunction of what appears on lines 5 and 8.

Exercise 7-2

The "strategy hints" from this chapter of the study guide should get you through these problems. I will make a few comments on some of these below which may be of further help if you are having trouble with them.

(1) Remember to use EI before UI as the "strategy hints" suggest.

(5) Again, remember to use EI before UI. The first half of the conclusion can be derived from the first two premises. The second half can be derived from the third premise, but you will have to use UI on it. Quantifiers cannot just be changed.

(7) When you use UI on the first premise, instantiate all of the bound z's with a's. In general, use whatever individual symbol will make the resulting line look as much as possible like other lines in the argument or proof whenever you use UI.

(9) Again, about the only way to really go wrong with this proof is to fail to use EI before UI.

Exercise 7-3

(1) Remember that you cannot use EI on parts of line 1. QN on line 2 will allow you to separate the conclusion from line 1 by DS.

(3) Use IMPL on the conclusion to see what you really need to derive. Then use QN on the premise and instantiate the resulting quantifier.

(5) Use QN on the second premise, and then use EI before UI.

(7) Use QN on the second premise and on the conclusion to see what you are looking for and how to obtain it.

(9) The second premise is absolutely useless, thrown in just to make the proof look more difficult than it really is. Just ignore it and the proof is quite easy.

(11) Use EI before UI, and the rest of the problem is just a lot of sentential logic.

(13) Use both possible assumed premises, (x)(Sx ⊃ Px) and Sx, and then derive Rx. Use CP, UG and CP again and the proof is complete.

Exercise 7-4

The text warns you that "some of these are rather difficult", and a similar warning from Chapter Four should have prepared you to take this one seriously. The last few problems in this exercise are very difficult. I will try to provide some helpful comments below.

(1) You do not need to use an assumed premise for this proof at all. Just use EI before UI, and when all the quantifiers have been removed, you should have no trouble coming up with the conclusion.

(3) Once you have made the necessary QN moves, the only problem is one of deciding what to substitute for x when you make each of the three UI moves. The rule of thumb to follow in each case is to make some part of the premise look exactly like some part of the conclusion or some part of an already instantiated premise. Following this rule will lead to the following substitutions:

first premise	e for x
second premise	f for x
third premise	b for x

(5) Use both possible assumed premises, Fx and Nx.

(7) This looks terrible, but really isn't. Use the obvious assumed premise, $\sim(\exists y)(Gy \vee Lx)$. After using QN on the assumed premise, just instantiate everything. Remember to substitute the same variable for the x in line 1 and the y in line 2, otherwise you will not be able to derive the conclusion. You could even use x for every UI move, which would result in Ex • Nxx, from which you could derive $(\exists z)(Ez • Nzx)$ by EG. CP and UG would then complete the proof. If you do not do all the instantiations with x, you will need to use something other than x for the x in line 1 and the y in line 2 when you use UI on them.

(9) This looks terrible and it really is. The obvious assumed premise, $(\exists y)(Ay • Cxy)$ won't work. The x will be free in an EI line as soon as you remove that quantifier, and you will never be able to use UG to derive the conclusion and complete the proof. What you need to do is to use CONTRA on everything after the initial quantifier in the conclusion. Then use the antecedent of that conditional as your assumed premise and all will go well. It is still a fairly long and difficult derivation, and you were not expected to come up with it easily.

Exercises for Chapter Seven

Exercise 7-1 (Identifying Errors in Proofs of Validity)

Find and identify the errors in each of the following proofs of validity.

(1) 1. (∃x)Ax ⊃ (y)By   p

   2. (y)(Cy · Ay)   p

   3. Ax ⊃ (y)By   1, EI

   4. Ax ⊃ Bx   3, UI

   5. Cx · Ax   2, UI

   6. Ax   5, Simp

   7. Bx   4,6 MP

   8. Ax · Bx   6,7 Conj

   9. (y)(Ay · By)   8, UG

(2) 1. (∃y)(Hy · Fy)   p

   2. (x)[Fx ⊃ (∃y)Gy]   p

   3. (x)(Fx ⊃ Gy)   2, EI

   4. Fy ⊃ Gy   3, UI

   5. Hy · Fy   1, EI

   6. Fy   5, Simp

   7. Gy   4,6 MP

   8. Hy   5, Simp

   9. Gy · Hy   7,8 Conj

  10. (∃x)(Gx · Hx)   9, EG

(3) 1. $(x)(y)(Bxy \supset Ayx)$ p

     2. $(x)Bxx$ p

     3. $(x)(Bxx \supset Axx)$ 1, UI

     4. Bxx 2, UI

     5. $(x)Axx$ 3,4 MP

     6. Axy 5, UI

     7. $(\exists y)Axy$ 6, EG

     8. $(\exists x)(\exists y)Axy$ 7, EG

(4) 1. $(\exists y)(x)(z)Bxyz$ p

     2. $(x)(z)Bxyz$ 1, EI

     3. $(z)Bxyz$ 2, UI

     4. $Bxyz$ 3, UI

     5. $(\exists z)Bxzz$ 4, EG

     6. $(y)(\exists z)Byzz$ 5, UG

     7. $(x)(y)(\exists z)Byzx$ 6, UG

(5) 1. $(\exists x)(\exists y)Ayx$ p

     2. $(x)(y)(Axy \supset Byx)$ p

     3. $(\exists y)Ayx$ 1, EI

     4. Axy 3, EI

     5. $(y)(Axy \supset Byx)$ 2, UI

     6. $Axy \supset Byx$ 5, UI

     7. Byx 4,6 MP

     8. $(\exists x)Byx$ 7, EG

     9. $(\exists x)(\exists y)Byx$ 8, EG

Exercise 7-2   (Proofs of Validity without Quantifier Negation)

Prove the following arguments valid.

(1) 1. $(x)(Fx \supset Gx)$

    2. $Hh \supset Fg$ $/\therefore\ Hh \supset Gg$

(2) 1. $(y)[By \supset (\sim Ay \supset Ca)]$

    2. $\sim Ab$ $/\therefore\ Bb \supset Ca$

(3) 1. $\sim Oa$

    2. $(x)(y)[(Mx \vee Py) \supset (Oa \vee Ob)]$ $/\therefore\ Ma \supset Ob$

(4) 1. $(x)(y)(Fxy \cdot Fya)$ $/\therefore\ Faa$

(5) 1. $(\exists y)(My \cdot Ny)$

    2. $(z)(Nz \supset Pz)$ $/\therefore\ (\exists x)(Mx \cdot Px)$

(6) 1. $(x)[(Ax \cdot Bx) \supset (\exists y)Cy]$

    2. $(\exists y)(Ay \cdot By)$ $/\therefore\ (\exists z)Cz$

(7) 1. $(y)Ay \cdot (y)\sim By$

    2. $(\exists y)(Ay \cdot \sim By) \supset (x)Cx$ $/\therefore\ (y)Cy$

(8) 1. $(x)[Fx \vee (\exists y)Gy]$

    2. $(\exists x)\sim Fx$ $/\therefore\ (\exists x)Gx$

(9) 1. $(\exists x)Bx \supset (y)\sim Cy$

    2. $(y)(By \cdot Ay)$ $/\therefore\ (x)Ax \cdot (x)\sim Cx$

(10) 1. $(y)(Ay \supset \sim By)$

   2. $(\exists x)(Ax \cdot Cx)$

   3. $(y)Dy \supset \sim(\exists x)\sim Bx$ $/\therefore \sim(y)Dy$

(11) 1. $(x)\sim Px$

   2. $(\exists y)\sim Ly$

   3. $(x)[(Mx \lor Nx) \supset (Lx \lor Px)]$ $/\therefore (\exists y)\sim My$

(12) 1. $(x)(y)(Mxa \supset Oay)$ $/\therefore (y)(Mya \supset Oay)$

(13) 1. $(\exists x)(y)(Fxy \supset Gyx)$ $/\therefore (x)(\exists y)(Fyx \supset Gxy)$

(14) 1. $(\exists x)(y)(z)Azyx$ $/\therefore (x)(y)(\exists z)Axyz$

(15) 1. $(\exists y)(x)Mxy$

   2. $(y)(z)(Mzy \supset \sim Nyz)$ $/\therefore (y)(\exists x)\sim Nxy$

Exercise 7-3 (Proofs of Validity with Quantifier Negation)

   Prove the following arguments valid.

   (1) 1. $(y)(Fy \cdot \sim Gy)$ $/\therefore \sim(\exists y)(Fy \supset Gy)$

   (2) 1. $(y)(Ay \supset \sim By)$ $/\therefore \sim(\exists y)(Ay \cdot By)$

   (3) 1. $(x)[(Mx \lor Nx) \supset Ox]$

   2. $(y)(Py \supset My)$ $/\therefore \sim(\exists x)(Px \cdot \sim Ox)$

(4) 1. $(\exists x)(y)Fxyx$ $/\therefore \sim(x)(\exists y)\sim Fxyx$

(5) 1. $\sim(\exists x)\sim Mx$

    2. $(y)[(My \cdot Oy) \supset Py]$ $/\therefore (x)(Ox \supset Px)$

(6) 1. $(\exists x)Fx$

    2. $(y)[Fy \supset (\sim Gy \supset \sim Hy)]$

    3. $\sim(\exists y)(Fy \cdot \sim Hy)$ $/\therefore (\exists x)Gx$

(7) 1. $(x)[(Mx \cdot Nx) \supset Ox]$

    2. $(y)(Py \supset My)$

    3. $\sim(\exists x)\sim Px$ $/\therefore \sim(\exists x)(Nx \cdot \sim Ox)$

(8) 1. $(\exists x)(y)\sim Fxy$ $/\therefore \sim(x)Fxa$

(9) 1. $\sim(y)(\exists x)\sim(Bxy \cdot Byx)$ $/\therefore (\exists x)Bxx$

(10) 1. $(\exists x)(y)(\sim Axy \supset Ayx)$ $/\therefore \sim(x)(y)\sim Axy$

(11) 1. $(x)(y)\sim Gxy$

    2. $(\exists y)(x)(Fx \supset Gyx)$ $/\therefore \sim(x)Fx$

(12) 1. $(\exists x)(y)(Cx \supset \sim Byx)$

    2. $\sim(\exists y)(\exists x)\sim Bxy$ $/\therefore \sim(y)Cy$

(13) 1. $(\exists x)(y)Axy$

    2. $(x)(\exists y)(Axy \supset \sim Bxx)$ $/\therefore \sim(y)Byy$

(14) 1. $(x)(\exists y)(Fxy \supset \sim Gyx)$

    2. $(\exists y)(x)Fyx$ $/\therefore (\exists x)(\exists y)\sim Gxy$

(15) 1. $(\exists y)(x)(Fx \supset Gxy)$

    2. $(y)(\exists x)\sim Gxy$ $/\therefore (\exists y)\sim Fy$

CHAPTER EIGHT

Predicate Logic--III

1 Invalidity in Predicate Logic

The text shows you two methods for demonstrating the invalidity of
arguments in predicate logic. The first makes use of expansions of each
of the sentences in an argument into a universe consisting of two
individuals. The second involves finding a clearly invalid argument,
that is, one which we know has true premises and a false conclusion,
having exactly the same form as the argument in question. Although
there are invalid arguments in predicate logic which would require the
second of these methods in order to show them invalid, this is not the
case with any of the invalid arguments in the text. And the problem
with this second method is that if your imagination comes up empty,
there is really nothing you can do. And there is not any easy way to
quickly increase your ability in this area. So I recommend that you use
the first method whenever you have any trouble demonstrating the invalidity of arguments in predicate logic. It is sufficient to demonstrate
the invalidity of any of the examples discussed in the text or contained
in Exercise 8-1. What you must do to employ it is the following:

> (1) Expand each sentence in the argument (premises and conclusion)
>   into a universe of discourse consisting of two individuals.

> (2) Treat the expanded argument just as you did in sentential
>   logic. Show that a set of truth values can be assigned to the
>   atomic sentences in the expansions so that all of the premises
>   come out true and the conclusion false.

If you have any questions about how to construct the expansions referred
to in (1) above, look back at the instructions in Chapter Six of this
study guide. If you have any questions about the process mentioned in
(2) above, refer to the section on invalidity in Chapter Five.

2 Consistency and Inconsistency of Premises

As was the case in sentential logic, demonstrating that the premises of an argument in predicate logic are consistent is just like
demonstrating that the argument is invalid, except that we simply ignore
the argument's conclusion. Either of the methods discussed at the
beginning of the previous section can be used to do this, the point
being to show that all of the premises of the argument could be true.
And, as before, expansions of the premises into a universe of discourse
consisting of two individuals is sufficient to demonstrate the consistency of the premises for any of the arguments used as examples in the
text or contained in Exercise 8-2.

Demonstrating the inconsistency of premises in predicate logic is done in exactly the same way as it was in sentential logic. Just use the valid argument forms (of both sentential and predicate logic) to show that an explicit contradiction, that is, a sentence or formula of the form p·~p, can be derived from the premises of the argument. As before, since the inconsistency of the premises alone is to be demonstrated, no assumed premises whatsoever can be used in the process. Do not confuse this with the technique of indirect proof.

3   Translation of More Difficult Sentences in Predicate Logic

This section is a continuation of the sections dealing with translation in Chapter Six. It deals with the translation of more complicated sentences from English into the symbolic notation of predicate logic. The complication involved is of two sorts. The first consists of a number of special constructions which you will have to learn to translate. The second involves sentences with multiple quantifiers of overlapping scope which are much more complex than those covered at the end of Chapter Six. I will try to give you some help in dealing with both of these sources of difficulty.

Special Constructions

"None but", "only" and "unless" are covered quite thoroughly in the text. In general, sentences containing these constructions are translated using the universal quantifier as follows:

(1) "Only F's are G" = $(x)(Gx \supset Fx)$ (for example, "Only fools are gullible")

(2) "None but the = $(x)(Gx \supset Fx)$ (for example, "None but the fool is
F is/are G"   gullible")

(3) "None are G unless = $(x)(\sim Fx \supset \sim Gx)$ (for example, "None are gull-
they are F"   ible unless they are fools")

All of the above translations could be obtained by changing everything after the universal quantifier into the form of an "unless" or "only if" sentence about x, treating x as though it were a constant, and translating this transformed sentence just as you would have in sentential logic. ("None but" is the same as "only" in English.)

There is an exception to the general rules above for translating these special constructions. It involves sentences which cannot be translated using the universal quantifier. Almost every sentence which begins with "some" or "there is/are" will require the existential quantifier and so cannot have material implication as its major connective. In such cases, the "only" and "unless" which appear in these sentences are to be confined within compound predicates, giving the internal structure of the predicates rather than the overall structure of the entire formula following the quantifier. So, for example, the sentence:

"Some people are happy only when drunk"

is translated: $(\exists x)[Px \cdot (Hx \supset Dx)]$

where the material in the parentheses corresponds to the compound predicate "x is happy only if x is drunk" and the major connective of the entire formula following the quantifier is still conjunction as it should be. Similarly, the sentence:

"Some people are not happy unless they are drunk"

is translated: $(\exists x)[Px \cdot (\sim Dx \supset \sim Hx)]$

where the material in the parentheses corresponds to the compound predicate "x is not happy unless x is drunk".

Sometimes connectives such as "and" and "or" appear to connect predicates but actually connect whole sentences. For example, the sentence:

"Fruits and vegetables are nutritious"

does not say that things which are both fruits and vegetables are nutritious, and so cannot be translated as:

$$(x)[(Fx \cdot Vx) \supset Nx]$$

What this sentence really says is both that all fruits are nutritious and that all vegetables are nutritious, and so should be translated as:

$$(x)(Fx \supset Nx) \cdot (x)(Vx \supset Nx)$$

This is also the same as saying that anything which is either a fruit or a vegetable is nutritious, so it could also be translated as:

$$(x)[(Fx \lor Vx) \supset Nx]$$

Similarly, the sentence:

"Students are neither all popular nor all logical"

which could be put into this form:

"It is not the case that students are either all popular or all logical"

does not say that it is false that all students are either popular or logical, and so cannot be translated as:

$$\sim(x)[Sx \supset (Px \lor Lx)]$$

125

What this setence really says is that it is false either that all
students are popular or that all students are logical, and so should be
translated as:

$$\sim[(x)(Sx \supset Px) \vee (x)(Sx \supset Lx)]$$

This is also the same as saying that it is false that all students are
popular and false that all students are logical, so it could also be
translated as:

$$\sim(x)(Sx \supset Px) \cdot \sim(x)(Sx \supset Lx)$$

Multiple Quantifiers of Overlapping Scope

Sentences involving more than one quantifier need not be much more
difficult to translate than sentences with a single quantifier. The
trick is to translate these sentences one quantifier at a time. In
general, this can be done as follows.

(1) Use the general translation technique from Chapter Six of this
study guide to obtain the initial quantifier, the subject of
the sentence for purposes of translation (not necessarily the
grammatical subject), and the major connective of the entire
formula following the initial quantifier.

(2) At this point the remaining quantifier(s) will be included in
what the sentence predicates or says is true of its subject.
Translate this entire predicate as though it were a separate
sentence, pretending that the initial quantifier variable is a
constant within this smaller sentence. That is, identify the
subject for purposes of translation of this smaller sentence,
its quantifier and major connective, proceeding as in (1)
above but regarding the initial quantifier variable as though
it were a constant.

(3) If there are more than two quantifiers in the sentence, continue as in (2) above, pretending at each stage of the process that all previous quantifier variables are constants.

I will illustrate this technique for dealing with multiple quantifiers
with an example. To translate the sentence:

"Every student fails at least one exam"

(1) The sentence is about students, and about all rather than just
some of them, so it's translation will begin:

$$(x)[Sx \supset$$

(2) What is predicated of every student, x, by this sentence is
that they fail at least one exam. So the predicate is the
smaller sentence, "x fails at least one exam", with x to be

regarded here as though it were a constant for purposes of translation.

So the subject of this smaller sentence is exams, the first kind of thing that this sentence talks about some or all of (since x is treated as a constant here). And the sentence is about some (at least one), not all exams. So this smaller sentence's translation will begin:

$$(\exists y)(Ey \cdot$$

And the smaller sentence predicates of some exams that they are failed by x, so its predicate is Fxy, and the entire smaller sentence's translation is:

$$(\exists y)(Ey \cdot Fxy)$$

Inserting this into the partial translation of the entire sentence from step (1), we obtain the following correct translation of the complete sentence with which we started:

$$(x)[Sx \supset (\exists y)(Ey \cdot Fxy)]$$

The choice of a different quantifier variable in the second step of the process above is automatic, because the first quantifier variable is regarded as a constant at this point.

There are two advantages to translating complicated sentences with multiple quantifiers in the manner illustrated above. First, it reduces the complexity at each stage of the process to that involved with single quantifier sentences. Second, by placing each of the quantifiers at the point in the sentence at which they 'naturally' occur, it allows you to check the correlation between kind of quantifier and the major connective following it which the general rules for translation in Chapter Six of the study guide describe. And this will save you from many mistranslations of difficult sentences.

4   Theorems of Logic

The discussion of theorems of logic in Section 4 of the text is quite clear. If you read it carefully, you should have no difficulty with this material. The example at the bottom of p.146 is not quite so clear, however. What needs to be added is this. Since what is being proved is a particular substitution instance of Rule QN, Rule QN cannot itself be used anywhere in the proof. That is why so much ingenuity is required to construct it. None of the problems in Exercise 8-5 has this feature. For each of them, all of the valid argument forms of sentential and predicate logic may be used to demonstrate that it is indeed a theorem of logic.

5 Proofs of Validity in Predicate Logic with Identity

Adding Rule ID to the other argument forms of predicate logic is a fairly simple matter. You should not have much trouble with any of the proofs in Exercise 8-6 in the text. A few of the problems in Exercise 8-3 at the end of this chapter of the study guide are quite difficult, however. The last two proofs in that exercise are meant to be a challenge, and are at least as difficult as any of the proofs in the previous chapter of the text.

Remember that Rule ID is an implicational argument form. The identity statement which allows you to make substitutions in some line of a proof must itself be a complete line of that proof. Notice, also, that Rule ID only permits you to substitute the right-hand member of an identity statement for the left hand member in a proof. So, from Fa and a = b we can derive Fb by the use of Rule ID. But we cannot go directly from Fb and a = b to Fa by using Rule ID, even though the inference involved would clearly be valid. If you want to make such a move, here is how to get around the one-sidedness of Rule ID in such cases:

1.	Fb	p
2.	a = b	p
→3.	~Fa	AP
4.	~Fb	2,3 ID
5.	Fb · ~Fb	1,4 Conj
6.	Fa	3-5 IP

The strategy demonstrated above can be generalized so that it can be used whenever you want to substitute the left-hand for the right-hand member of an identity statement in any proof. I should add, however, that you will never really need to make use of this strategy. That is, although it is available to you and may be convenient at some point, it is never necessary to substitute the left-hand member for the right-hand member of an identity statement in order to complete a proof.

There is one more important restriction on the use of Rule ID in addition to those just discussed above. The symbol which you substitute for, that is, the one which is replaced, by Rule ID must be free at every point in the line at which you make the substitution. This is especially important when substituting for variables in a proof. You cannot change the identity of bound variables or of quantifier variables by Rule ID.

Students are sometimes tempted to use Rule ID 'backwards'. There is no way to derive the negation of an identity statement directly by the use of this rule. You cannot, for example, make a move like the following:

```
        •
        •
        •
   m.   Fa

   n.   ~Fb

   o.   ~(a = b)                              m,n ID
```

So whenever the conclusion of an argument is the negation of an identity statement and that identity statement (or an identity statement which could be turned into that one by instantiation or substitution of identicals) occurs nowhere in the premises of the argument, the only way to complete the proof is by using the technique of indirect proof.

6 Translation in Predicate Logic with Identity

The translation of sentences involving identity can be quite difficult. Be sure that you give Sections 5 and 6 of this chapter of the text some long and very careful study. Keep in mind that the examples on pp.151-153 of the text are using a restricted domain of discourse. That is not true of the translation exercises on this material either in the text or in this study guide. When you encounter such sentences without this restriction on the domain of discourse, you will have to make use of the predicate Px ("x is a person") and produce more complicated translations for sentences like these.

Sentences whose translation requires the identity symbol can be divided into three general kinds. The first consists of sentences which are essentially like those encountered in Section 3 of this chapter, except that they involve the use of an identity symbol. For example:

"Everyone loves someone else"

is just like the sentence "Everyone loves someone (or other)", and we have already encountered many sentences of this general form, except that it involves an additional piece of information which can only be translated by using the identity symbol. The correct translation of the above sentence is:

$$(x)\{Px \supset (\exists y)[(Py \cdot Lxy) \cdot (x \neq y)]\}$$

Such sentences present no unique translation problems at all. The skills required to translate them are the same as those required for translating sentences like those in Exercise 8-3 of the text. All that identity does in the case of such sentences is allow us to express more detailed information in terms of what the sentence predicates of its

129

subject.

The second general kind of sentences whose translation involves identity consists of sentences which deal with quantities other than none, some or all of a given kind of thing. These sentences contain "at least", "at most" or "exactly" together with some number and are discussed at length in the text. I will give an example of each of these quantity constructions and its translation, and comment briefly on how the translation works.

Consider the sentence:

"Art loves at least two people"

The first thing to do in translating sentences like this is to get clear about just what the sentence says there are "at least" some number of. One way to do this is to rewrite such sentences so that they begin with the quantity construction, "There is/are at least...", as illustrated below:

"There are at least two people Art loves"

This shows us that both being a person and being loved by Art will have to be built into the description contained in the translation of the "at least two" construction for this sentence. The entire sentence can be translated as follows:

$$(\exists x)(\exists y)\{[(Px \cdot Lax) \cdot (Py \cdot Lay)] \cdot (x \neq y)\}$$

I will try to suggest what the various parts of the translation above are actually designed to accomplish. There seem to be at least two different things which are both persons and loved by Art. That is the point of the existential quantifiers and descriptions which follow them. And they really are different things, so there are, in fact, at least two of them. That is the point of the non-identity statement following the descriptions.

We can generalize loosely from this example in a way that would apply to all "at least" sentences as follows. Any sentence which says that there are at least some number of things which fit a certain description will be translated by that same number of existential quantifiers and complete descriptions written in terms of their quantifier variables, followed by a sufficient number of non-identity statements to rule out the possibility that any two of those variables are in fact identical. All of the parts of the translation will be connected by the symbol for conjunction. If the number following "at least" is one, no non-identity statements are required, of course, because there are not any pairs of variables which could possibly be identical.

Now consider the sentence:

"Art loves at most two people"

It is useful to rewrite this sentence as we did the previous one, so as to show the complete description of the kind of thing the sentence says there are "at most" some number of.

"There are at most two people that Art loves"

This shows us that both being a person and being loved by Art will have to be built into the description contained in the translation of the "at most two" construction for this sentence. The entire sentence can be translated as follows:

$$(x)(y)\{\{[(Px \cdot Lax) \cdot (Py \cdot Lay)] \cdot (x \neq y)\} \supset (z)\{(Pz \cdot Laz) \supset [(z = x) \vee (z = y)]\}\}$$

Once again, I will try to suggest what the various parts of this translation are actually designed to accomplish. There may not be anything which fits the complete description "is both a person and loved by Art". That is the point of the conditional formula following the initial quantifiers. Anytime we do find two different things which fit that description (that is the point of the universal quantifiers, the two descriptions which follow them, and the non-identity statement), we will discover that every apparent third thing that fits the description (that is the point of the third universal quantifier and description following it) is really identical to one of the first two (that is the point of the disjunction of identity statements) so that there really are, in fact, at most two such things.

As before, we can generalize loosely from this example in a way that will apply to all "at most" sentences. Any sentence which says that there are at most some number of things which fit a certain description will be translated by that same number of universal quantifiers, complete descriptions written in terms of their quantifier variables, and a sufficient number of non-identity statements to rule out the possibility that any two of those variables are in fact identical, followed by the symbol for material implication. The consequent of the translation will consist of one more universal quantifier and a conditional formula whose antecedent is the complete description written in terms of its quantifier variable and whose consequent is the disjunction of identity statements containing that same variable and each of the initial quantifier variables in turn. If the number following "at most" is one, no non-identity statements are required, of course, and since there will be only one pair of variables in the translation, the consequent of the consequent will consist of a single identity statement rather than a disjunction of such statements.

Now, finally, consider the sentence:

"Art loves exactly two people"

Again it is useful to rewrite the sentence so as to show the complete description of the kind of thing the sentence says there are "exactly" some number of.

"There are exactly two people that Art loves"

This shows us that both being a person and being loved by Art are to be included in the description of the kind of thing the sentence says there are exactly two of. The sentence can be translated as follows:

$$(\exists x)(\exists y)\{\{[(Px \cdot Lax) \cdot (Py \cdot Lay)] \cdot (x \neq y)\} \cdot (z)\{(Pz \cdot Laz) \supset [(z = x) \vee (z = y)]\}\}$$

As before, I will try to suggest what the various parts of the translation above actually accomplish. The first half of the translation is identical to the translation of the sentence "There are at least two people Art loves", and that is the information it conveys. The last half of the sentence tells us that every time we think we have found another person loved by Art (that is the point of the universal quantifier and description following it), it will turn out that this apparent third person is identical to one of the first two (that is the point of the disjunction of identity statements), so that there are, in fact, at least two such persons and no more, that is, exactly two persons loved by Art.

Generalizing from this example as we did in the case of the previous constructions yields the following. Any sentence which says that there are exactly some number of things which fit a certain description will be translated by that same number of existential quantifiers, complete descriptions written in terms of their quantifier variables, and a sufficient number of non-identity statements to rule out the possibility that any two of those variables are in fact identical, followed by the symbol for conjunction. The second conjunct of the translation will consist of a universal quantifier and a conditional formula whose antecedent is the complete description written in terms of the universal quantifier variable and whose consequent is the disjunction of identity statements containing that same variable and each of the existential quantifier variables in turn. If the number following "exactly" is one, no non-identity statements are required, of course, and since there will be only one pair of variables in the translation, the consequent of the formula following the universal quantifier will consist of a single identity statement rather than a disjunction of such statements.

The third general kind of sentences whose translation involves identity consists of sentences containing definite descriptions. There are actually two kinds of definite descriptions, that is, descriptions which identify an individual thing because it is the one and only thing fitting the description. The first kind uses the definite article ("the") and a set of predicates which together are true of one and only one thing. For example:

"the exam John failed"

is a definite description of this kind. Such definite descriptions are the same for purposes of translation as "exactly" sentences of the sort discussed above. For "the exam John failed" to be a proper definite description, there must be exactly one thing which is an exam failed by John. And that can be translated as follows:

132

$$(\exists x)\{(Ex \cdot Fjx) \cdot (y)[(Ey \cdot Fjy) \supset (y = x)]\}$$

When such a definite description is used in a sentence, it should be translated just as I have done above, and then whatever the sentence predicates of the thing described should be conjoined to the description. So, for example, the sentence:

"The exam John failed was not difficult"

would be translated as follows:

$$(\exists x)\{\{(Ex \cdot Fjx) \cdot (y)[(Ey \cdot Fjy) \supset (y = x)]\} \cdot \sim Dx\}$$

The second kind of definite description uses comparative properties to identify the one object which has the most or the one object which has the least of the property according to which the things are compared. So, for example, we could pick out a single object with the description:

"the most intelligent student"

or with the description:

"the least intelligent student"

These descriptions are translated by indicating that there is at least one of the kind of things being compared, in this case students:

$$(\exists x)Sx$$

and then going on to say that all **other** students are less or more intelligent than this one, as follows:

$$(\exists x)\{Sx \cdot (y)\{[Sy \cdot (y \neq x)] \supset Ixy\}\} \text{ and}$$

$$(\exists x)\{Sx \cdot (y)\{[Sy \cdot (y \neq x)] \supset Iyx\}\}$$

for "the most intelligent student" and "the least intelligent student" respectively. As with the previous kind of definite description, you would then conjoin to the description whatever the sentence containing it predicated of the thing so described.

Discussion of Exercises from Text

Exercises 8-1 & 8-2

Review the material in Sections 1 and 2 of both text and study guide if you have questions about how to do any of the problems in these exercises. Remember that invalidity and premise consistency can be demonstrated by expansions into a two-individual universe for any of the arguments in these exercises if you are unable to think of appropriate arguments having the same form.

Exercise 8-3

Almost everyone has some trouble with the worst of the translations in this exercise. Review carefully the material in Chapter Six and Section 3 of Chapter Eight of this study guide if you are having a great deal of trouble.

Exercise 8-4

When you have determined the truth conditions of these sentences, be sure that you express them in colloquial English. If you really understand the information that these sentences convey, you should be able to express it in a way that would not cause your roommate to wonder what you were trying to tell her.

Exercise 8-5

Remember that all of the valid argument forms of sentential and predicate logic may be used on these problems. Remember also that the proof of theorems whose major connective is material equivalence will typically involve two separate conditional proofs to establish the material implication version of the theorem in both directions. The theorem itself can then be derived by using Conj and then Equiv on the results of those conditional proofs.

Exercise 8-6

The difficulty of these problems has little to do with Rule ID. It is plain old predicate logic difficulty. Review the discussion and "strategy hints" from Chapter Seven of this study guide.

Exercise 8-7

Review very carefully the discussion in the last section of this chapter of the study guide, especially the material on translating definite descriptions, if you have trouble with this exercise.

Exercises for Chapter Eight

Exercise 8-1   (Translation in Predicate Logic)

Bx = "x is boring"	Dxy = "x is more difficult than y"
Cx = "x is a course"	Ixy = "x is more interesting than y"
Dx = "x is demanding"	Kxy = "x knows y"
Ex = "x is an exam"	Pxy = "x passes y"
Gx = "x is good"	Txy = "x takes y"
Px = "x is a person"	
Qx = "x is a quiz"	j = "John"
Sx = "x is a student"	m = "Mary"

Symbolize the following sentences, using the predicate and individual constants above.

1. There are students who don't know anything.

2. No student knows everything.

3. Some students pass every quiz they take.

4. No student passes every exam she takes.

5. Good students pass every course they take.

6. Every good student takes at least one demanding course.

7. Mary is a good student, but she doesn't pass every exam she takes.

8. There are students and courses that are not boring.

9. John takes every course that Mary passes.

10. Every student takes some of the courses that John takes.

11. No courses are taken by everyone.

12. Quizzes and exams are demanding.

13. Quizzes are more interesting than exams.

14. Boring courses are more difficult than demanding ones.

15. No one is more interesting than John.

16. Good students won't take boring courses.

17. Some students don't take any courses that are more interesting than the courses John takes.

18. The exams Mary doesn't pass are more difficult than any of the exams John takes.

19. No one passes all the exams John takes.

20. There are demanding courses that are more interesting than any boring course.

21. Some students will take any course that isn't demanding.

22. Mary knows everything and everyone that John knows.

23. Only good students take demanding courses.

24. Mary doesn't take a course unless it is a good one.

25. Mary takes courses only if they are more difficult than the courses John takes.

26. John passes all of the exams he takes unless they are demanding.

27. Only good students pass every course they take.

28. Good students won't take courses unless they are demanding.

29. John won't take any course unless Mary does too.

30. Mary won't take a course unless it is both more difficult and more interesting than any of the courses John has passed.

Exercise 8-2 (Translation in Predicate Logic)

Translate the following sentences into English, being as colloquial as possible. The constants have the same meanings as in Exercise 8-1 above.

1. $\sim(\exists x)[Px \cdot (y)Kxy]$

2. $(x)[Px \supset (\exists y)\sim Kxy]$

3. $(x)[Px \supset \sim(y)Kxy]$

4. $(x)[Px \supset (\exists y)(Sy \cdot Kxy)]$

5. $\sim(\exists x)[Px \cdot (y)(Sy \supset Kxy)]$

6. $(x)[Sx \supset (\exists y)(Ey \cdot \sim Pxy)]$

7. $(\exists x)[Sx \cdot \sim(\exists y)Kxy]$

8. $(x)[Px \supset (\exists y)(Py \cdot Kxy)]$

9. $\sim(\exists x)[Px \cdot (y)(Py \supset Kxy)]$

10. $\sim(\exists x)[Px \cdot (\exists y)Kxy]$

11. $\sim(\exists x)[Px \cdot (\exists y)(Kxy \cdot \sim Kjy)]$

12. $(x)[Px \supset \sim(y)(Kmy \supset Kxy)]$

13. $(\exists x)[Sx \cdot \sim(\exists y)(Ey \cdot Pxy)]$

14. $\sim(\exists x)\{Sx \cdot (y)[(Ey \cdot Txy) \supset Pxy]\}$

15. $(x)\{Sx \supset (\exists y)[(Dy \cdot Ey) \cdot Pxy]\}$

Exercise 8-3   (Proofs of Validity in Predicate Logic with Identity)

Prove the following arguments valid.

(1) 1. $(x)(y)[(x = y) \supset Bxy]$

    2. $(x)(y)(Byx \supset Ay)$

    3. $\sim Aa$ $/\therefore \sim(a = b)$

(2) 1. $(\exists x)Gx$

    2. $(y)(z)[(Fy \cdot Gz) \supset (y = z)]$ $/\therefore Fa \supset (\exists x)(a = x)$

(3) 1. $(\exists x)(\exists y)(x = y) \supset (z)Az$

    2. $a = b$ $/\therefore Ab$

(4) 1. $Fc \supset \sim Gc$

    2. $(x)(Fx \supset Gb)$ $/\therefore Fc \supset \sim(b = c)$

(5) 1. $(\exists x)Gx$

    2. $(x)(y)(x = y)$ $/\therefore (x)(Fx \supset Gx)$

(6) 1. $(\exists x)(\exists y)(x = y) \supset (x)Mx$

    2. $\sim Ma$ $/\therefore \sim(b = c)$

(7) 1. $a = b$

    2. $(\exists x)(Ax \cdot \sim Bx) \supset (x)(y)\sim(x = y)$ $/\therefore Ac \supset Bc$

(8) 1. $(x)(Ax \supset Ba)$

    2. Aa

    3. $Ab \supset \sim Bb$ $/\therefore \sim(a = b)$

(9) 1. $(x)(y)[Axy \supset (x = y)]$

    2. Ba

    3. $(x)(y)(By \supset Axy)$ $/\therefore\ a = b$

(10) 1. $(\exists x)(\exists y)(x = y) \supset (z)(Fz \supset Gz)$

    2. $b = c$ $/\therefore\ Fb \supset Gc$

(11) 1. $(x)(y)(Mxy \supset Nyx)$

    2. $(\exists x)(\exists y){\sim}(x = y) \supset (\exists x)(\exists y)Myx$

    3. ${\sim}(x)(y)(Ox \supset Oy)$ $/\therefore\ (\exists x)(\exists y)Nxy$

(12) 1. $(x)(Fx \lor {\sim}Fx)$ $/\therefore\ (x)(y)(z)\{[(x = y) \lor (x = z)] \lor (y = z)\} \supset$
$\{[(x)Fx \lor (x)(Fx \supset Gx)] \lor (x)(Fx \supset {\sim}Gx)\}$

Exercise 8-4 (Translation in Predicate Logic with Identity)

Ex = "x is an exam"   Dxy = "x is more difficult than y"
Sx = "x is a student"   Fxy = "x fails y"
                            Ixy = "x is more intelligent than y"
g = "George"   Wxy = "x does well on y"

     Symbolize the following sentences, using the predicate and
individual constants above.

1. There is at least one student who will do well on every exam.

2. George is more intelligent than at least two other students.

3. There are at least two exams that George will do well on.

4. There are at least two students who are not more intelligent than
George.

5. Only George does well on every exam.

6. George is the only student who fails any exams.

7. George will do well on one exam at most.

8. There are at most two exams that George will fail.

9. George will not fail the least difficult exam.

10. Only George will fail the least difficult exam.

11. George is not the most intelligent student.

12. The student who will do well on the most difficult exam is not George.

13. George did well on exactly two exams.

14. The exam George failed was not the most difficult exam.

15. If George is the most intelligent student, he will do well on the most difficult exam.

ANSWERS TO EVEN-NUMBERED ITEMS

Chapter One

Exercise 1-1

2.a. Yes, as long as the argument has at least one false premise.

   b. Yes, validity does not require that the premises be true. Of course, the argument will be unsound if any of its premises is false, but it can still be valid.

   c. Yes. A valid argument can have false premises. And if the premises are false, validity places no restriction on the possible truth value of the conclusion. The conclusion of a valid argument with one or more false premises can be either true or false.

   d. No. This is the one combination of actual truth values which is ruled out by validity.

   e. Yes, if it has at least one false premise.

4.a. Yes. In fact, **only** valid arguments can be sound. Sound **means** valid and all premises true as well.

   b. No.

   c. No. See 4.a.

   d. No. A sound deductive argument is one which both is valid and has all true premises. And a valid deductive argument with true premises must have a true conclusion. That is what validity means.

Exercise 1-2

2. e.	8. c.
4. a.	10. a.
6. e.	

Chapter Two

Exercise 2-1

2. Yes, this sentence is a conjunction. When it is split into the two sentences "John is allergic to penicillin" and "John is allergic to ragweed", those sentences together convey the same meaning as did the original sentence.

4. No, this sentence is not a conjunction. If we split it into the two sentences "Russia is supposed to be an enemy" and "The United States is supposed to be an enemy", we lose the fact that they are supposed to be enemies of each other. And that was part of the meaning of the original sentence.

6. No, this sentence is not a conjunction. If we split it into the two sentences "The Grand Inquisitor thought that freedom was incompatible" and "The Grand Inquisitor thought that bread enough for all was incompatible", we produce sentences that don't make much sense and we also lose the fact that the Grand Inquisitor thought these two things to be incompatible with each other. The original sentence did make sense and did include that fact as part of its meaning.

8. No, this sentence is not a conjunction. The sentence means that no one voted for both Carter and Reagan in 1980. It certainly does not mean that no one voted for Carter and that no one voted for Reagan in that year, which is what we would convey if we turned that sentence into a conjunction of two sentences.

10. Yes, this sentence is a conjunction. When it is split into the two sentences "Carter has tried to bring about an end to hostilities in the Middle East" and "Reagan has tried to bring about an end to hostilities in the Middle East", those sentences together convey the same meaning as did the original sentence.

12. No, this sentence is not a conjunction. The sentence means that oil and vinegar together make up a single popular salad dressing. It certainly does not mean that each one of those by itself is a popular salad dressing, and so cannot be treated as the conjunction of two sentences.

14. Yes, this sentence is a conjunction. When it is split into the two sentences "Reagan was victorious in 1980" and "Bush was victorious in 1980", those sentences together capture all of the meaning of the original sentence.

Exercise 2-2

Since the skill required for this exercise and the next has already been discussed at length in this study guide, all that will be provided here are the answers and the values of the variables which turn each form into a picture of the sentence it matches.

2.   a -- p=B

4.   a -- p=~B · A
     c -- p=~B, q=A
     e -- p=B, q=A

6.   a -- p=~~A
     b -- q=~A

8.   a -- p=~(A · ~B)
     b -- q=A · ~B
     d -- p=A, q=~B
     i -- p=A, q=B

10. a -- p=~[A · (~B ∨ ~C)]
     b -- q=A · (~B ∨ ~C)
     d -- p=A, q=~B ∨ ~C
     k -- p=A, q=~B, r=~C
     l -- p=A, q=B, r=~C

Exercise 2-3

2.   a -- p=~B
     b -- p=B

4.   a -- p=A ⊃ B
     c -- p=A, q=B

6.   a -- p=~(A ⊃ B)
     b -- p=A ⊃ B
     g -- p=A, q=B

8.   a -- p=~[A ⊃ (B ⊃ C)]
     b -- p=A ⊃ (B ⊃ C)
     g -- p=A, q=B ⊃ C
     k -- p=A, q=B, r=C

Chapter Three

Exercise 3-1

2. S ⊃ T.   Remember that the "if" sentence always comes first in a
            conditional sentence, regardless of where it occurs in
            the sentence in English.

4. L • ~R. The "and so" in this sentence has the same truth-functional
            meaning as a simple "and". Both of these sentences must be
            true (L and ~R) in order for the compound sentence to be
            true, and that makes it a conjunction.

6. ~(T ∨ P). This sentence could also be translated ~T • ~P as the
             "translation hints" indicate.

8. P ⊃ T.   Remember that the "only if" reverses the order from what it
            would have been for a simple "if" sentence of this form like
            sentence 2 above. Also, this sentence cannot be translated
            as a material equivalence sentence. The sentence in English
            is clearly true. However, the reverse implication which the
            material equivalence connective would add to the literal
            meaning of the sentence, T ⊃ P, is clearly false. John could
            translate this sentence correctly and still not do this
            entire exercise perfectly. In fact, he could mistranslate
            every other sentence for all we know.

10. S ⊃ ~D. This is a conditional sentence in English which lacks
             the usual English indications of its form, "if" or "in
             case". You can tell that it is a conditional by substi-
             tuting "If John had" for "Had John" and noting that the
             meaning of the sentence is unchanged by so doing. There
             is another possible complication with this sentence due
             to its tense and mood. It is possible for this sentence
             to be used not just to convey the conditional sentence
             shown above as its correct translation, but also to imply
             that (unfortunately) John did not study very diligently
             and did find the sentence too difficult to translate.
             And that would require translating it as (S ⊃ ~D) • (~S • D).

12. W ≡ (S • R). The only possible problem with this sentence is its
                  grouping. The discussion of punctuation or grouping
                  on pp.22-23 tells you how to group this sentence
                  correctly using the order in which the English con-
                  nective words appear.

14. (T ∨ ~W) ⊃ (~S ∨ ~R). As with the previous sentence, grouping is the
                           only possible source of difficulty here, and
                           the instructions in this study guide are suf-
                           ficient to enable you to determine the correct
                           grouping.

16. $L \equiv D$. Remember that "just in case" has the same meaning as "if and only if".

18. $(S \cdot \sim D) \supset T$. The order of the English connective words in this sentence indicates its correct grouping.

20. $\sim L \equiv \sim T$. Remember that because of the nature of the material equivalence relation, this could also be translated as $\sim T \equiv \sim L$, $L \equiv T$, or $T \equiv L$. The reason that it should be translated as material equivalence rather than material implication is that the reverse implication can be put in this form: "If John looks at the answers in the back of the book, then he will translate this sentence correctly". And, since that is clearly true, the sentence should be translated in terms of the "broader meaning" which includes this additional implication.

Exercise 3-2

2. Either my Buick or my Triumph will start.

4. It is not the case that both my Buick and my Triumph will start.

6. If my Buick won't start, I'll send it back to the junkyard.

8. If neither my Buick nor my Triumph will start, then I'll either ride my bike or walk.

10. I'll walk if and only if there is a flat tire on my bike.

12. If neither my Buick nor my Triumph will start and there is a flat tire on my bike, then I'll have to walk. (Of course, you do not need to use the "neither...nor..." construction to translate the first part of the antecedent of this sentence.)

14. I'll walk only if my bike has a flat tire, and I'll send my Buick back to the junkyard only if it won't start. (Of course, you do not need to use the "only if" construction here at all.)

16. If my Triumph won't start but I still don't walk, then either my bike doesn't have a flat tire or I didn't send my Buick back to the junkyard and it will start.

18. I'll send my Buick back to the junkyard if and only if it won't start, but it's not true that I'll walk if and only if I don't ride my bike.

20. I am definitely not going to walk, and so if neither my Triumph nor my Buick will start, I'll ride my bike even if it has a flat tire.

Exercise 3-3

2. Contradictory

4. Tautologous

6. Tautologous

8. Contingent

10. Contingent

In addition to the answers above, I will show you an example of
what the work would look like which yields those answers if you follow
my earlier recommendation and use complete truth tables rather than
truth table analysis for these sentences. I will work with sentence 6
as my example: $\sim(A \supset B) \supset (A \equiv \sim B)$

A	B	~B	A ⊃ B	~(A ⊃ B)	A ≡~B	~(A ⊃ B) ⊃ (A ≡~B)
T	T	F	T	F	F	T
T	F	T	F	T	T	T
F	T	F	T	F	T	T
F	F	T	T	F	F	T

Since the final column of this truth table has a T in every
row, the sentence is tautologous.

Chapter Four

Exercise 4-1

(2) 4. 1,2 HS
    5. 3,4 HS

(4) 5. 3,4 DS
    6. 1,5 MP
    7. 3.6 MP
    8. 2,7 MT

(6) 5. 3,4 HS
    6. 1,2,5 CD

(8) 5. 3, Add
    6. 4,5 MP
    7. 6, Simp
    8. 7, Add
    9. 1,8 MP
    10. 7, Add
    11. 2,10 MP
    12. 9,11 Conj
    13. 6, Simp
    14. 12,13 Conj

Exercise 4-2

(2) Incorrect use of Simp on line 4: this is an implicational form and cannot be used on part of a line; in this case, the antecedent of the conditional sentence on line 1.

(4) Incorrect use of MP on line 5: MP requires the antecedent of the conditional sentence exactly as it appears in the conditional sentence. Add must be used to obtain B ∨ C from B before MP can be used.

Incorrect use of DS on line 7: DS gives you half of a disjunction if you already have the negation of the other half. From lines 5 and 6, nothing follows by DS.

Incorrect use of MT on line 8: MT requires the negation of the consequent of a conditional sentence. You would need to have ~~E instead of ~E on line 7 before MT could be used here.

Incorrect use of Add on line 9: Add would give you ~E ∨ D.

Incorrect use of MP on line 10: this would be correct if line 4 were (~E · D) ⊃ C. But the location of its parentheses makes it a very different sentence and MP cannot be used here.

(6) Incorrect use of DS on line 6: to use DS, you would need ~~A instead of A on line 5.

Incorrect use of Add on line 8: Add would give you B ∨ A. B · A could have been obtained here from lines 5 and 7 by Conj.

Incorrect use of Conj on line 10: Conj is an implicational form,
and so cannot be used on part (the second conjunct) of line 6.

Exercise 4-3

   (2) 4. ~H   2,3 DS

       5. ~(F ∨ G)   1,4 MT

   (4) 4. T · R   2,3 DS

       5. R   4, Simp

       6. S   1,5 MP

       7. T   4, Simp

       8. S · T   6,7 Conj

   (6) 3. ~A   2, Simp

       4. ~A ∨ B   3, Add

       5. ~C ⊃ D   1,4 MP

       6. ~D   2, Simp

       7. ~~C   5,6 MT

   (8) 4. ~F   3, Simp

       5. G ⊃ I   1,4 MP

       6. ~H   3, Simp

       7. G   2,6 MP

       8. I   5,7 MP

       9. I ∨ K   8, Add

(10) 4. P ⊃ R   2,3 HS

     5. P ⊃ (S • ~T)   1,4 HS

(12) 5. S ∨ T   4, Add

     6. ~P   3,5 MP

     7. ~Q   1,6 DS

     8. ~R   2,7 MT

     9. ~R ∨ T   8, Add

(14) 4. ~D • E   1,2 MP

     5. ~D   4, Simp

     6. A   3,5 DS

     7. E   4, Simp

     8. A • E   6,7 Conj

(16) 4. (F ∨ G) ⊃ J   1,3 HS

     5. (F ∨ G) ⊃ (K • I)   2,4 HS

(18) 4. ~H   3, Simp

     5. ~H ∨ I   4, Add

     6. F • G   1,5 MP

     7. G   6, Simp

     8. K   2,7 MP

     9. ~J   3, Simp

     10. ~J • K   8,9 Conj

(20) 5. $F \supset (G \lor I)$ 1,3 HS

      6. $(G \lor I) \supset L$ 2,4 HS

      7. $F \supset L$ 5,6 HS

Exercise 4-4

(2) 2. 1, DN
     3. 2, Add
     4. 3, Impl
     5. 4, Add
     6. 5, Comm
     7. 6, Impl

(4) 5. 1,2 MT
     6. 5, DeM
     7. 6, Simp
     8. 4,7 MP
     9. 6, Simp
    10. 3,9 DS
    11. 8,10 Conj
    12. 11, DeM
    13. 12, DN
    14. 13, Impl

(6) 4. 2, DeM
     5. 4, Impl
     6. 5, DN
     7. 3,6 HS
     8. 7, Exp
     9. 8, Comm
    10. 9, Exp
    11. 1, Exp
    12. 11, Comm
    13. 12, Exp
    14. 6,13 HS
    15. 14, Exp
    16. 15, Taut
    17. 10,16 HS
    18. 17, Exp
    19. 18, Taut
    20. 19, Impl
    21. 20, Comm
    22. 21, DN
    23. 22, DeM

Exercise 4-5

(2) Incorrect use of Contra on line 5: line 5 should read $\sim G \supset \sim F$ if Contra is used. To obtain $\sim F \supset G$, $G \supset F$ would have had to have been obtained instead of $F \supset G$ from line 3 by Simp.

Incorrect use of Impl on line 7: when going from a disjunction to a material implication sentence, Impl requires that a negation sign be dropped. So DN would have to be used on line 6 to obtain $\sim\sim G \lor \sim H$ before Impl could be used to obtain line 7 of this proof.

(4) Incorrect use of Equiv on line 5: Equiv would have yielded $(A \cdot B) \lor (\sim A \cdot \sim B)$.

Incorrect use of DN on line 6: DN would have yielded $\sim C \lor D$.

Incorrect use of Exp on line 8: Exp cannot be used on line 1 at all. Exp can only be used on conditional sentences which have conjunctions as antecedents or conditionals as consequents, not vice versa.

Incorrect use of Contra on line 10: line 9 would have to be ~A ⊃ ~B before Contra could be used to obtain line 10.

Incorrect use of DeM on line 12: DeM would have yielded ~D v ~E.

Incorrect use of Impl on line 13: Impl would have yielded ~B v (A · C).

Incorrect use of Dist on line 14: Dist cannot be used as long as there is a negation sign in front of (A · C) in line 13. If there were no negation sign there in line 13, Dist would have yielded (~B v A) · (~B v C).

Incorrect use of Simp on line 15: Simp is an implicational form and so can only be used on conjunctions which are complete lines of a proof.

Incorrect use of DeM on line 18: DeM would have yielded ~(A v E).

Exercise 4-6

(2) 3. ~(F ⊃ G) v ~(G ⊃ F)   1, Add

4. ~[(F ⊃ G) · (G ⊃ F)]   3, DeM

5. ~(F ≡ G)   4, Equiv

(4) 3. ~R · ~S   1, DeM

4. ~R   3, Simp

5. ~R v ~U   4, Add

6. ~(R · U)   5, DeM

7. ~T   2,6 MT

8. ~T v W   7, Add

9. T ⊃ W   8, Impl

(6) 3.   N   2, Simp

4.   ~~N   3, DN

5.   ~~N v ~O   4, Add

6.   ~(~N · O)   5, DeM

7.   ~M   1,6 MT

8.   ~M v L   7, Add

9.   M ⊃ L   8, Impl

(8) 3.   ~~F v (G · ~H)   1, Impl

4.   (~~F v G) · (~~F v ~H)   3, Dist

5.   ~~F v ~H   4, Simp

6.   ~F ⊃ ~H   5, Impl

7.   H ⊃ F   6, Contra

8.   H   2, Simp

9.   F   7,8 MP

10. F v ~G   9, Add

11. ~G v F   10, Comm

12. G ⊃ F   11, Impl

(10) 4. ~S · ~T   2, DeM

5. ~W v (R · U)   3, Impl

6. (~W v R) · (~W v U)   5, Dist

7. ~W v R   6, Simp

8. ~S   4, Simp

9. ~R   1,8 MT

10. ~W   7,9 DS

(12) 3. $(\sim R \supset S) \cdot (S \supset \sim R)$ 1, Equiv

     4. $\sim\sim R \vee \sim T$ 2, DeM

     5. $S \supset \sim R$ 3, Simp

     6. $\sim R \supset \sim T$ 4, Impl

     7. $S \supset \sim T$ 5,6 HS

     8. $\sim S \vee \sim T$ 7, Impl

     9. $\sim(S \cdot T)$ 8, DeM

     10. $\sim(T \cdot S)$ 9, Comm

(14) 3. $\sim\sim I$ 2, DN

     4. $\sim\sim I \vee \sim H$ 3, Add

     5. $\sim(\sim I \cdot H)$ 4, DeM

     6. $\sim(H \cdot \sim I)$ 5, Comm

     7. $\sim(F \cdot \sim G)$ 1,6 MT

     8. $\sim F \vee \sim\sim G$ 7, DeM

     9. $\sim F \vee G$ 8, DN

     10. $F \supset G$ 9, Impl

(16) 3. $(\sim B \vee A) \cdot (\sim B \vee \sim C)$ 1, Dist

     4. $\sim B \vee \sim C$ 3, Simp

     5. $B \supset \sim C$ 4, Impl

     6. $\sim D \supset \sim C$ 2,5 HS

     7. $C \supset D$ 6, Contra

(18) 4. $[H \supset (F \lor G)] \cdot [(F \lor G) \supset H]$ 2, Equiv

       5. $\sim G \cdot \sim I$ 3, DeM

       6. $\sim G$ 5, Simp

       7. $\sim F \cdot \sim G$ 1,6 Conj

       8. $\sim (F \lor G)$ 7, DeM

       9. $H \supset (F \lor G)$ 4, Simp

      10. $\sim H$ 8,9 MT

      11. $\sim H \lor I$ 10, Add

      12. $H \supset I$ 11, Impl

(20) 3. $\sim R$ 2, Simp

       4. $\sim R \lor \sim P$ 3, Add

       5. $\sim P \lor \sim R$ 4, Comm

       6. $\sim (P \cdot R)$ 5, DeM

       7. $\sim (O \cdot M)$ 1,6 MT

       8. $\sim O \lor \sim M$ 7, DeM

       9. O 2, Simp

      10. $\sim\sim O$ 9, DN

      11. $\sim M$ 8,10 DS

      12. $\sim M \lor N$ 11, Add

      13. $M \supset N$ 12, Impl

Chapter Five

Exercise 5-1

(2)   No incorrect move has been made, but leaving the proof at this
      point shows a misunderstanding of the way assumed premises work.
      No proof is complete which has an open assumption, that is, an
      assumed premise which has not been used in either CP or IP. Once
      F is assumed, the only way to complete the proof is to obtain G on
      a line and then use CP to obtain F ⊃ G. This proof could be com-
      pleted with one step of MP and one step of CP to obtain F ⊃ G with-
      out any open assumptions.

(4)   For indirect proof, the assumed premise must be the negation of
      the conclusion. So the correct assumption in this case would be
      ～～(C · D). Also, as in problem 2 above, reaching the conclusion
      without having used the assumed premise in CP or IP does not
      complete a proof. With the correct AP, this proof could be
      completed from line 9 in two steps, first using Conj on lines 4
      and 9 to obtain an explicit contradiction, and then using IP to
      obtain the conclusion.

(6)   The strategy used in this proof is the correct one for an argu-
      ment with a material equivalence sentence as its conclusion.
      For such arguments you should think of the conclusion as two
      separate conditional sentences, obtain each of them by a sepa-
      rate conditional proof, and then use Conj and Equiv to obtain
      the conclusion. However, this particular proof involves a
      serious mistake in the way in which that basic strategy is
      carried out. Because the work which is done on the second and
      third premises between lines 5 and 10 of the proof is within
      the scope of the first assumption, it cannot be used once that
      assumption is closed off by CP at line 13. So the use of Impl
      at line 15 is incorrect. Once you reach line 13, lines 4 thru
      12 of the proof are closed off and cannot be used again. The
      way around this problem in such proofs is to do whatever work
      is required on the premises before starting either of the con-
      ditional proofs, thus making these lines available throughout
      the entire proof.

Exercise 5-2

```
    | 5.   H                               2,4 MP
    | 6.   G ⊃ H                           3-5 CP
      7.   F ⊃ (G ⊃ H)                     2-6 CP


(4)▶2.   F ⊃ ~G                            AP
     3.   ~F ∨ ~G                          2, Impl
   | 4.   ~(F · G)                         3, DeM
     5.   (F ⊃ ~G) ⊃ ~(F · G)             2-4 CP


(6)▶2.   G                                 AP
     3.   G ∨ ~F                           2, Add
     4.   ~F ∨ G                           3, Comm
   | 5.   F ⊃ G                            4, Impl
     6.   G ⊃ (F ⊃ G)                      2-5 CP
     7.   ~G ∨ (F ⊃ G)                     6, Impl
```

Notice that in both problem 4 and problem 6 above the premises of the arguments were in fact irrelevant. Both arguments have tautologous conclusions, and that is why those conclusions could be obtained by conditional proof without making use of the given premises.

```
(8)▶3.   ~P                                AP
     4.   ~(~M ∨ O)                        2, Impl
     5.   ~~M · ~O                         4, DeM
     6.   ~~M                              5, Simp
     7.   M                                6, DN
     8.   M ∨ N                            7, Add
     9.   O                                1,8 MP
    10.   ~O                               5, Simp
   | 11.   O · ~O                          9,10 Conj
```

155

12.	P	3-11 IP

(10)➤3.	~~N	AP
4.	N	3, DN
5.	N ∨ O	4, Add
6.	M	1,5 MP
7.	M • ~M	2,6 Conj
8.	~N	3-7 IP

(12)➤3.	M	AP
4.	~~M	3, DN
5.	~(O • P)	2,4 MT
6.	~O ∨ ~P	5, DeM
7.	O ⊃ ~P	6, Impl
8.	N ⊃ ~P	1,7 HS
9.	~N ∨ ~P	8, Impl
10.	M ⊃ (~N ∨ ~P)	3-9 CP

(14)➤4.	~O	AP
5.	M ⊃ N	2,4 MP
6.	~~M	3,4 MT
7.	M	6, DN
8.	N	5,7 MP
9.	N ⊃ O	1,7 MP
10.	O	8,9 MP
11.	O • ~O	4,10 Conj
12.	O	4-11 IP

(16)▶3. ~~H   AP

   4. H   3, DN

   5. ~G ⊃ F   2,4 MP

   6. ~~G ∨ F   5, Impl

   7. G ∨ F   6, DN

   8. F ∨ G   7, Comm

   9. (F ∨ G) • ~(F ∨ G)   1,8 Conj

  10. ~H   3-9 IP

(18)▶5. ~0   AP

   6. ~L ⊃ ~P   2,5 MP

   7. ~(~P ∨ Q)   3, Impl

   8. ~~P • ~Q   7, DeM

   9. ~~P   8, Simp

  10. ~~L   6,9 MT

  11. L   10, DN

  12. ~(M ∨ N)   1,11 MP

  13. ~M • ~N   12, DeM

  14. ~Q   8, Simp

  15. ~~(L ⊃ M)   4,14 MT

  16. L ⊃ M   15, DN

  17. M   11,16 MP

  18. ~M   13, Simp

  19. M • ~M   17,18 Conj

  20. 0   5-19 IP

```
(20)►2.  R ∨ S                                                      AP

  ►3.  R ⊃ S                                                        AP

    4.  ∼∼R ∨ S                                                     2, DN

    5.  ∼R ⊃ S                                                      4, Impl

    6.  ∼S ⊃ ∼R                                                     3, Contra

    7.  ∼S ⊃ S                                                      5,6 HS

    8.  ∼∼S ∨ S                                                     7, Impl

    9.  S ∨ S                                                       8, DN

   10.  S                                                           9, Taut

   11.  (R ⊃ S) ⊃ S                                                 3-10 CP

   12.  (R ∨ S) ⊃ [(R ⊃ S) ⊃ S]                                     2-11 CP

  ►13.  (R ⊃ S) ⊃ S                                                 AP

   14.  ∼(R ⊃ S) ∨ S                                                13, Impl

   15.  ∼(∼R ∨ S) ∨ S                                               14, Impl

   16.  (∼∼R · ∼S) ∨ S                                              15, DeM

   17.  (R · ∼S) ∨ S                                                16, DN

   18.  S ∨ (R · ∼S)                                                17, Comm

   19.  (S ∨ R) · (S ∨ ∼S)                                          18, Dist

   20.  S ∨ R                                                       19, Simp

   21.  R ∨ S                                                       20, Comm

   22.  [(R ⊃ S) ⊃ S] ⊃ (R ∨ S)                                     13-21 CP

   23.  {(R ∨ S) ⊃ [(R ⊃ S) ⊃ S]} · {[(R ⊃ S) ⊃ S] ⊃ (R ∨ S)}      12,22 Conj

   24.  (R ∨ S) ≡ [(R ⊃ S) ⊃ S]                                     23, Equiv
```

Exercise 5-3

2.a. Yes.

b. Yes. In fact, an invalid argument must have consistent premises. Any deductive argument with inconsistent premises is valid, as this chapter of the study guide explained.

c. Yes, if it is valid and if its premises are all true. Remember that consistency just means that the premises could all be true, not that they are actually all true.

d. Yes, if it is either invalid or has at least one false premise.

4.a. No. Consistency means that they could be true, that is, that they do not contain contradictory information. It does not mean that they are true.

b. No. It must have a true conclusion only if its premises are actually all true.

c. No. It will be sound only if its premises are true, and consistency does not require that.

d. No, it could be unsound, but it does not have to be.

e. Yes.

f. Yes.

6.a. Yes, if it has at least one false premise. Remember that consistency does not rule out the having of false premises. It only rules out contradictory (logically false) premises.

b. Yes.

c. Yes, as long as it is invalid.

d. Yes.

e. No. If it were sound it would be valid and have true premises. And any valid argument with true premises would have to have a true conclusion as well.

f. Yes, in fact it would have to be unsound. No sound argument has a false conclusion.

Exercise 5-4

(2) This argument can be shown to be invalid by demonstrating that its premises would be true and its conclusion false if F, G and H were all true. The truth table analysis below does this.

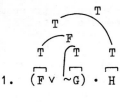

1. (F ∨ ~G) · H

2. G ≡ H

3. ~H ⊃ ~G   /∴ G ⊃ ~H

(4) This argument can be shown to be invalid by demonstrating that its premises would be true and its conclusion false if G were true and both F and H false. The truth table analysis below does this.

1. H ⊃ G

2. ~G ⊃ ~F

3. ~ [(G ⊃ H) ∨ F]   /∴ G ⊃ (H · F)

Exercise 5-5

(2) 4.	~S ∨ W	3, Comm
5.	S ⊃ W	4, Impl
6.	S ⊃ T	1,5 HS
7.	(S ⊃ T) · ~(S ⊃ T)	2,6 Conj

(4) 4.	(~R ⊃ T) · (T ⊃ ~R)	2, Equiv
5.	T ⊃ ~R	4, Simp
6.	T ⊃ S	1,5 HS
7.	(T ⊃ S) · ~(T ⊃ S)	3.6 Conj

Exercise 5-6

(2) The premises are consistent because they would all be true if A, B and C were all false, as demonstrated in the truth table analysis below.

1.

2.

3.

(4) The premises are consistent because they would all be true if A and C were true, and B false, as demonstrated in the truth table analysis below.

1.

2.

161

3. $\overset{\displaystyle T}{\overbrace{\underset{T}{C} \equiv \overset{T\quad F}{\underset{\sim B}{}}}}$

Chapter Six

Exercise 6-1

2. Vs · ~Ks

4. (Fk · Fm) · Fs

6. ~(Vk ∨ Kk)

8. (Fks · Fsk) · (Fke · Fse)

10. ~(Cse ∨ Cme) · Cke

Exercise 6-2

2. McCoy is fond of Spock even though Spock is unemotional.

4. Spock will command the Enterprise, but McCoy won't.

6. Neither Kirk nor McCoy are Vulcans, but Spock is.

8. Neither Kirk nor McCoy are hostile aliens.

10. Kirk, McCoy and Spock are all fond of one another and of the Enterprise.

Exercise 6-3

2. $(x)[(Bx \cdot Cx) \supset {\sim}Ix]$

4. $(\exists y)[(Iy \cdot Cy) \cdot {\sim}Dy]$

6. $\sim(\exists x)[Sx \cdot (Ix \cdot Bx)]$

8. $(\exists y)[(By \cdot Sy) \cdot Kgy]$

10. $(x)[(Ex \cdot Tmx) \supset Pmx]$

12. $(z)(Sz \supset Kzg)$

14. $(\exists y)[Sy \cdot (Kyj \cdot {\sim}Kym)]$

16. $\sim(x)Kgx$

18. $\sim(y)[(Cy \cdot Tjy) \supset Pjy]$

20. $(x)(Kjx \supset Lgxj)$

Exercise 6-4

2. Difficult courses are not boring.

4. Some difficult courses aren't interesting.

6. There are courses which are neither interesting nor difficult.

8. No courses are difficult.

10. John doesn't know any interesting students.

12. George has taken some boring courses.

14. John learned something from Mary.

16. John hasn't passed every exam he's taken.

18. John doesn't pass every course that Mary passes.

20. George learned everything he knows from Christina.

Exercise 6-5

2. ~Ba ∨ ~Bb

4. (Fa · ~Ha) ∨ (Fb · ~Hb)

6. ~(Fa ∨ Ga) ∨ ~(Fb ∨ Gb)

8. (Maa · Mba) ∨ (Mab · Mbb)

10. (Maa · Mba) · (Mab · Mbb)

12. (Maa · Mba) ∨ (Mab · Mbb)

14. [(Fa ⊃ Gaa) ∨ (Fa ⊃ Gab)] · [(Fb ⊃ Gba) ∨ (Fb ⊃ Gbb)]

16. (Maaa ∨ Mbaa) · (Maab ∨ Mbab)

Chapter Seven

Exercise 7-1

(2) 1. The inference to line 3 is invalid. EI is an implicational argument form and cannot be used on part of line 2.

2. The inference to line 5 is invalid. y cannot be used in EI at this point because it has already occurred free in the proof on lines 3 and 4.

(4) 1. The inference to line 5 is invalid. Two different kinds of free symbols have been bound by the added quantifier.

2. The inference to line 7 is invalid. The symbol that has become bound by the added quantifier was not free in line 6.

Exercise 7-2

(2) ►3. Bb   AP

4. Bb ⊃ (~Ab ⊃ Ca)   1, UI

5. ~Ab ⊃ Ca   3,4 MP

6. Ca   2,5 MP

7. Bb ⊃ Ca   3-6 CP

(4) 2. (y)(Fay · Fya)   1, UI

3. Faa · Faa   2, UI

4. Faa   3, Taut

(6) 3. Ax · Bx   2, EI

4. (Ax · Bx) ⊃ (∃y)Cy   1, UI

5. (∃y)Cy   3,4 MP

6. Cw   5, EI

7.	(∃z)Cz	6, EG

(8) 3.   ~Fx   2, EI

      4.   Fx ∨ (∃y)Gy   1, UI

      5.   (∃y)Gy   3,4 DS

      6.   Gy   5, EI

      7.   (∃x)Gx   6, EG

(10) 4.   Ax · Cx   2, EI

      5.   Ax ⊃ ~Bx   1, UI

      6.   Ax   4, Simp

      7.   ~Bx   5,6 MP

      8.   (∃x)~Bx   7, EG

      9.   ~~(∃x)~Bx   8, DN

    10.   ~(y)Dy   3,9 MT

(12) 2.   (y)(Mxa ⊃ Oay)   1, UI

      3.   Mxa ⊃ Oax   2, UI

      4.   (y)(Mya ⊃ Oay)   3, UG

(14) 2.   (y)(z)Azyu   1, EI

      3.   (z)Azvu   2, UI

      4.   Awvu   3, UI

      5.   (∃z)Awvz   4, EG

      6.   (y)(∃z)Awyz   5, UG

      7.   (x)(y)(∃z)Axyz   6, UG

Exercise 7-3

(2) 2. $(y)(\sim Ay \lor \sim By)$ 1, Impl

     3. $(y)\sim(Ay \cdot By)$ 2, DeM

     4. $\sim(\exists y)(Ay \cdot By)$ 3, QN

(4) 2. $(\exists x)\sim(\exists y)\sim Fxyx$ 1, QN

     3. $\sim(x)(\exists y)\sim Fxyx$ 2, QN

(6) 4. $(y)\sim(Fy \cdot \sim Hy)$ 3, QN

     5. Fx 1, EI

     6. $Fx \supset (\sim Gx \supset \sim Hx)$ 2, UI

     7. $\sim Gx \supset \sim Hx$ 5,6 MP

     8. $Hx \supset Gx$ 7, Contra

     9. $\sim(Fx \cdot \sim Hx)$ 4, UI

     10. $\sim Fx \lor \sim\sim Hx$ 9, DeM

     11. $\sim Fx \lor Hx$ 10, DN

     12. $Fx \supset Hx$ 11, Impl

     13. Hx 5,12 MP

     14. Gx 8,13 MP

     15. $(\exists x)Gx$ 14, EG

(8) 2. $(y)\sim Fxy$ 1, EI

     3. $\sim Fxa$ 2, UI

     4. $(\exists x)\sim Fxa$ 3, EG

     5. $\sim(x)Fxa$ 4, QN

(10) 2. $(y)(\sim Axy \supset Ayx)$ 1, EI

3. $\sim Axx \supset Axx$ 2, UI

4. $\sim\sim Axx \vee Axx$ 3, Impl

5. $Axx \vee Axx$ 4, DN

6. Axx 5, Taut

7. $(\exists y)Axy$ 6, EG

8. $\sim(y)\sim Axy$ 7, QN

9. $(\exists x)\sim(y)\sim Axy$ 8, EG

10. $\sim(x)(y)\sim Axy$ 9, QN

(12) 3. $(y)\sim(\exists x)\sim Bxy$ 2, QN

4. $(y)(x)\sim\sim Bxy$ 3, QN

5. $(y)(Cw \supset \sim Byw)$ 1, EI

6. $Cw \supset \sim Bzw$ 5, UI

7. $(x)\sim\sim Bxw$ 4, UI

8. $\sim\sim Bzw$ 7, UI

9. $\sim Cw$ 6,8 MT

10. $(\exists y)\sim Cy$ 9, EG

11. $\sim(y)Cy$ 10, QN

(14) 3. $(x)Fwx$ 2, EI

4. $(\exists y)(Fwy \supset \sim Gyw)$ 1, UI

5. $Fwz \supset \sim Gzw$ 4, EI

6. Fwz 3, UI

7. $\sim Gzw$ 5,6 MP

8. $(\exists y)\sim Gzy$ 7, EG

9. $(\exists x)(\exists y)\sim Gxy$ 8, EG

Chapter Eight

Exercise 8-1

2. ~(∃x)[Sx · (y)Kxy]

4. ~(∃x){Sx · (y)[(Ey · Txy) ⊃ Pxy]}

6. (x){(Gx · Sx) ⊃ (∃y)[(Dy · Cy) · Txy]}

8. (∃x)(Sx · ~Bx) · (∃x)(Cx · ~Bx)

10. (x){Sx ⊃ (∃y)[(Cy · Tjy) · Txy]}

12. (x)(Qx ⊃ Dx) · (x)(Ex ⊃ Dx) or (x)[(Qx ∨ Ex) ⊃ Dx]

14. (x){(Bx · Cx) ⊃ (y)[(Dy · Cy) ⊃ Dxy]}

16. (x){(Gx · Sx) ⊃ (y)[(By · Cy) ⊃ ~Txy]}

18. (x){(Ex · ~Pmx) ⊃ (y)[(Ey · Tjy) ⊃ Dxy]}

20. (∃x){(Dx · Cx) · (y)[(By · Cy) ⊃ Dxy]}

22. (x)(Kjx ⊃ Kmx) · (x)[(Px · Kjx) ⊃ Kmx]

24. (x)[(Cx · ~Gx) ⊃ ~Tmx]

26. (x){[(Ex · Tjx) · ~Dx] ⊃ Pjx}

28. (x){(Gx · Sx) ⊃ (y)[(Cy · ~Dy) ⊃ ~Txy]}

30. (x){{Cx · ~(y)[(Cy · Pjy) ⊃ (Dxy · Ixy)]} ⊃ ~Tmx}

Exercise 8-2

2. No one knows everything.

4. Everyone knows at least one student.

6. No student passes every exam.

8. Everyone knows someone (or other).

10. No one knows anything.

12. No one knows everything that Mary knows.

14. No student passes every exam she takes.

Exercise 8-3

(2)►3.   Fa   AP

    4.   Gx   1, EI

    5. $(z)[(Fa \cdot Gz) \supset (a = z)]$ 2, UI

    6. $(Fa \cdot Gx) \supset (a = x)$ 5, UI

    7. $Fa \cdot Gx$ 3,4 Conj

    8. $a = x$ 6,7 MP

    9. $(\exists x)(a = x)$ 8, EG

   10. $Fa \supset (\exists x)(a = x)$ 3-9 CP

(4)►3. $\sim[Fc \supset \sim(b = c)]$ AP

    4. $\sim[\sim Fc \vee \sim(b = c)]$ 3, Impl

    5. $\sim\sim Fc \cdot \sim\sim(b = c)$ 4, DeM

    6. $\sim\sim Fc$ 5, Simp

    7. Fc 6, DN

    8. $\sim Gc$ 1,7 MP

    9. $Fc \supset Gb$ 2, UI

   10. Gb 7,9 MP

   11. $\sim\sim(b = c)$ 5, Simp

   12. $b = c$ 11, DN

   13. Gc 10,12 ID

   14. $Gc \cdot \sim Gc$ 8,13 Conj

   15. $Fc \supset \sim(b = c)$ 3-14 IP

(6) 3.   (∃x)~Mx   2, EG

     4.   ~(x)Mx   3, QN

     5.   ~(∃x)(∃y)(x = y)   1,4 MT

     6.   (x)~(∃y)(x = y)   5, QN

     7.   (x)(y)~(x = y)   6, QN

     8.   (y)~(b = y)   7, UI

     9.   ~(b = c)   8, UI

(8) ►4.   ~~(a = b)   AP

     5.   a = b   4, DN

     6.   Aa ⊃ Ba   1, UI

     7.   Ba   2,6 MP

     8.   Ab   2,5 ID

     9.   ~Bb   3,8 MP

     10. Bb   5,7 ID

     11. Bb · ~Bb   9,10 Conj

     12. ~(a = b)   4-11 IP

(10) 3.   (∃y)(b = y)   2, EG

     4.   (∃x)(∃y)(x = y)   3, EG

     5.   (z)(Fz ⊃ Gz)   1,4 MP

     6.   Fb ⊃ Gb   5, UI

     7.   Fb ⊃ Gc   2,6 ID

(12) ►2.   (x)(y)(z){[(x = y) ∨ (x = z)] ∨ (y = z)}   AP

    ►3.   ~[(x)Fx ∨ (x)(Fx ⊃ Gx)]   AP

    ►4.   Fu   AP

5.	$\sim(x)Fx \cdot \sim(x)(Fx \supset Gx)$	3, DeM
6.	$\sim(x)Fx$	5, Simp
7.	$(\exists x)\sim Fx$	6, QN
8.	$\sim Fv$	7, EI
9.	$\sim(x)(Fx \supset Gx)$	5, Simp
10.	$(\exists x)\sim(Fx \supset Gx)$	9, QN
11.	$\sim(Fw \supset Gw)$	10, EI
12.	$\sim(\sim Fw \lor Gw)$	11, Impl
13.	$\sim\sim Fw \cdot \sim Gw$	12, DeM
14.	$(y)(z)\{[(w = y) \lor (w = z)] \lor (y = z)\}$	2, UI
15.	$(z)\{[(w = v) \lor (w = z)] \lor (v = z)\}$	14, UI
16.	$[(w = v) \lor (w = u)] \lor (v = u)$	15, UI
→17.	$\sim\sim(v = u)$	AP
18.	$v = u$	17, DN
19.	$\sim Fu$	8,18 ID
20.	$Fu \cdot \sim Fu$	4,19 Conj
21.	$\sim(v = u)$	17-20 IP
22.	$(w = v) \lor (w = u)$	16,21 DS
→23.	$\sim\sim(w = v)$	AP
24.	$w = v$	23, DN
25.	$\sim\sim Fw$	13, Simp
26.	$\sim\sim Fv$	24,25 ID
27.	$\sim Fv \cdot \sim\sim Fv$	8,26 Conj
28.	$\sim(w = v)$	23-27 IP
29.	$w = u$	22,28 DS
30.	$\sim Gw$	13, Simp
31.	$\sim Gu$	29,30 ID

32.	Fu ⊃ ~Gu	4-31 CP
33.	(x)(Fx ⊃ ~Gx)	32, UG
34.	~[(x)Fx ∨ (x)(Fx ⊃ Gx)] ⊃ (x)(Fx ⊃ ~Gx)	3-33 CP
35.	~~[(x)Fx ∨ (x)(Fx ⊃ Gx)] ∨ (x)(Fx ⊃ ~Gx)	34, Impl
36.	[(x)Fx ∨ (x)(Fx ⊃ Gx)] ∨ (x)(Fx ⊃ ~Gx)	35, DN
37.	(x)(y)(z){[(x = y) ∨ (x = z)] ∨ (y = z)} ⊃ {[(x)Fx ∨ (x)(Fx ⊃ Gx)] ∨ (x)(Fx ⊃ ~Gx)}	2-36 CP

Exercise 8-4

2. (∃x)(∃y){{{[Sx · (x ≠ g)] · Igx} · {[Sy · (y ≠ g)] · Igy}} · (x ≠ y)}

4. (∃x)(∃y){[(Sx · ~Ixg) · (Sy · ~Iyg)] · (x ≠ y)}

6. [Sg · (∃x)(Ex · Fgx)] · (y){[Sy · (∃z)(Ez · Fyz)] ⊃ (y = g)}

8. (x)(y){{[(Ex · Fgx) · (Ey · Fgy)] · (x ≠ y)} ⊃ (z){(Ez · Fgz) ⊃ [(z = x) ∨ (z = y)]}}

10. (∃x){{{Ex · (y){[Ey · (y ≠ x)] ⊃ Dyx}} · Fgx} · (z)[Fzx ⊃ (z = g)]}

12. (∃x){{{Ex · (y){[Ey · (y ≠ x)] ⊃ Dxy}} · (∃z){{(Sz · Wzx) · (w)[(Sw · Wwx) ⊃ (w = z)]} · (z ≠ g)}}}

14. (∃x){{(Ex · Fgx) · (y)[(Ey · Fgy) ⊃ (y = x)]} · (∃z){{Ez · (w){[Ew · (w ≠ z)] ⊃ Dzw}} · (x ≠ z)}}